KAMTAPUR MOVEMENT IN BENGAL

KAMTAPUR MOVEMENT IN BENGAL

Dr. Rana Sonia Tez Bahadur

KALPAZ

First Published, 2019

Published by

Kalpaz Publications
C-30, Satyawati Nagar,
Delhi – 110052
Ph.: 011-47034999, 9811692060
www.kalpazpublications.com
E-mail: kalpaz@hotmail.com

Printed at: G. Print Process, Delhi

Cataloging in Publication Data—DK
Courtesy: D.K. Agencies (P) Ltd. <docinfo@dkagencies.com>

Bahadur, Rana Sonia Tez, author.
Kamtapur movement in Bengal / Dr. Rana Sonia Tez Bahadur.
pages cm
Includes bibliographical references.
ISBN 9789353241902

1. Rajbangsi (South Asian people)—India—Koch Bihar (District)—Politics and government. 2. Rajbangsi (South Asian people)—India—Koch Bihar (District)—Ethnic identity. 3. Koch Bihar (India : District)—Politics and government—20th century. I. Title.

LCC DS432.R25B34 2019 | DDC 954.14 23

To Mom...

Contents

Foreword

Ethnic identity and marginalization has been central to many ethnic movements throughout the world. Most of the struggles in recent times are characterized by the use of identity as a political ideology. It is considered as a tool for group mobilization in order to achieve certain goals which may be social, economic or political in nature. While primordial factors may constitute the foundation of identity construction its growth in the political realm is contingent upon historical and political events. Thus the first and foremost point is to understand the context of the identity formation and to explore and analyse development of the social and political movement for improving the condition of the group.

The identity formation of one such community spread over in and around Duars and Cooch Behar, the Rajbongsi presents a very interesting interplay of social and political history. First attempt towards solidarity of the group manifests in the caste movement, be it Kshatriya Movement or the demand for being recognised under scheduled tribe category. The movement shifted to political domain with the demand for separate state of Kamtapur. History of Kamtapur Movement is the history of struggle for recognition of their culture and their distinct identity. It is this distinctiveness which they perceive as the basis for their marginalisation and underdevelopment. The solution lies, according to them in the creation of separate state for the Rajbongsis, to be called Kamtapur.

For an understanding of any movement the larger socio political context cannot be set aside. What is the larger context in the case of Kamtapur Movement? How does one locate the movement within the context of Indian majoritarianism? What could be the response of the government towards such autonomy movements? India has experienced many such movements since its independence and responses of the government, both at the Union and the concerned state governments, during such movements have been varied. Depending on the circumstances and political expediency, the responses has been promotive, accommodative or repressive. The response of the government, in turn, has changed the course of action for the group spearheading the movement.

The present book Kamtapur Movement in Bengal is a comprehensive study of the Kamtapur Movement. It delves into the origin, development and the trajectory of the Movement. The different phases of the movement has been discussed and analysed by the author giving the readers deep insights in to the problem. It is notable for its academic excellence, theoretical richness, in depth analysis, and lucidity. I congratulate the author for her effort. I have no hesitation in recording that this book has enriched the literature on the Kamtapur Movement.

Professor Ranju R Dhamala
Dept of Political Science
Assam University
Silchar

Preface

Autonomy movements based on ethnic identity has emerged as a common feature of the political scenario today. Countries around the globe face challenge in terms of security and sovereignty from the ethnic groups that demand autonomy or secession along the ethnic lines. Such movements which are often marked by violence and counter-violence have caused immense human sufferings in the form of displacement, loss of live, molestation and economic setback. Since independence India has witnessed myriad of ethnicity based autonomy movements. The validity of the Linguistic Re-organization of the States (1956) has been challenged, time and again, by many ethnic communities demanding autonomy or secession from the Indian Union. The fact that state mechanisms such as grant of huge economic funds and signing of peace accords with the agitating ethnic group have failed to provide a permanent solution to such movements makes the situation even more alarming.

One such movement which is the focal point of the book is the 'Kamtapur Movement' in Cooch Behar district of West Bengal. The study of autonomy movements such as 'Kamtapur Movement' becomes relevant in so far as it enables us to understand a sense of discrimination intrinsic to minority cultural groups. Exploring measures where by the aspirations of these smaller community may be accommodated in the national framework of policy making has become paramount so as to keep the territorial integrity of the Indian Union intact. Accordingly the primary purpose of the book is to examine causes responsible for the demand by the Rajbongshi for a separate state out of West Bengal. To meet this purpose the historical background of the Kamtapur Movement is studied since every autonomy movement has its roots in the historical events occurred in the past. In order to explore the ethnic dimension of these movements together with the socio-economic factors that contribute to the outbreak of ethnicity based autonomy demands an attempt is further made to trace the identity formation of Rajbongshi in India. It is against this background that the book aims to focus on the nature and the present status of the Kamtapur Movement.

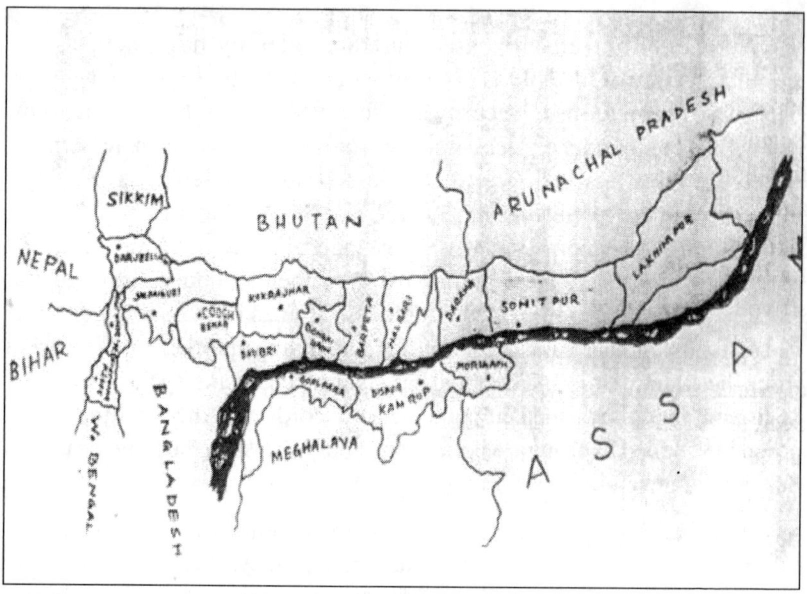

Source: Arup Jyoti Das, **Kamtapur and the Koch Rajbanshi Imagination**, Montage Media Publication, Assam, India, 2009, Pg. 13.

Figure 1 Map of the Proposed Kamtapur issued by All Koch Rajbongshi Student's Union

Acknowledgement

I would like to express my deep and sincere gratitude to my research supervisor, Professor Ranju R Dhamala, Head, Department of Political Science, Assam University, Silchar for providing invaluable guidance throughout my academic research. Her dynamism, sincerity, motivation and immense knowledge have deeply inspired me. It was a great privilege and honour to study under her guidance. I also offer my sincere gratitude for the learning opportunities provided by all my teachers as I continue to strive to be an ardent student of Political Science.

I am extending my heartfelt thanks to Shri Nikhil Roy, former member of Kamtapur People's Party and Shri Bangshi Badan Barman, General Secretary, The Greater Cooch Behar People's Association for discussing and sharing their incisive ideas on the Kamtapur movement in Coochbehar.

The completion of this book would not have been accomplished without the support of my family who toiled together with me to make this a reality. Finally, my gratitude goes to all the people who have directly or indirectly supported me in the accomplishment of this book.

Dr. Rana Sonia Tez Bahadur

Acknowledgement

[illegible]

Chapter - I

Ethnicity and Autonomy

Ethnicity: Meaning and Features

Ethnicity is a form of group allegiance that denotes personal identification involving a set of symbols or traits, which serve as the basis for this identification.[1] According to Horowitz, ethnicity as a term designates a sense of collective belonging, which could be based on common descent, language, history, culture, race, or religion.[2] It is centrally a matter of shared meanings conventionally called 'culture' but is also produced and reproduced during interaction.[3] Culture however can be loosely summarized as the complex of values, customs, beliefs and practices which constitute the way of life of a specific group. It is 'that complex whole', as anthropologist E B Tylor famously puts it in his *Primitive Culture* (1871), 'which includes knowledge, belief, art, morals, law, custom, and any other capabilities and habits acquired by man as a member of society.' Stuart Hall offers a similar view of culture as the 'lived practices' or 'practical ideologies which enable a society, group or class to experience, define, interpret and make sense of its conditions of existence.'[4] Ethnicity can thus mean 'the essence of an ethnic group' or 'the quality of belonging to ethnic community or group', generally in the context of (opposed) other ethnic groups.[5]

The two main patterns of *ethnie* formation that Anthony Smith identified are coalescence and division. Coalescence involves the coming together of separate units, which in turn can be broken down into processes of amalgamation of separate units such as city-states and of absorption of one unit by another as in the assimilation of regions. Division indicates subdivision through fission as with sectarian schism or through 'proliferation', when a part of the ethnic community leaves it to form a new unit as in the case of Bangladesh. *Ethnies*, to Smith, once formed tend to be exceptionally durable across history without undergoing any changes in their demographic composition and/or cultural contents. Smith pointed out that there are certain events that generate profound changes in the cultural contents of ethnic identities. He mainly singles out war and conquest, exile and enslavement, the influx of immigrants and religious conversion. He however suggests that what really matters is how far these changes reflect on and disrupt the sense of cultural continuity that binds successive generations together. For Smith, even the most radical changes cannot destroy this sense of continuity and common ethnicity. This is partly due to the existence of a number of external forces that help to crystallize ethnic identities and ensure their persistence over long periods. Of these, state-making, military mobilization and organized religion are the most critical.

Ethnic communities or *ethnies* commonly exhibit, albeit in varying degrees, six main features:

1. A common proper name, to identify and express the 'essence' of the community;
2. A myth of common ancestry, a myth rather than a fact, a myth that includes the idea of a common origin in time and place and that gives an *ethnie* a sense of fictive kinship, what Horowitz terms as 'super – family';
3. Shared historical memories or better, shared memories of a common past or pasts, including heroes, events, and their commemoration;
4. One or more elements of common culture, which need not be specified but normally include religion, customs, or language;
5. A link with a homeland, not necessarily its physical occupation by the *ethnie*, only its symbolic attachment to the ancestral land, as with diaspora peoples;
6. A sense of solidarity on the part of at least some sections of the *ethnie's* population.[6]

Attributes of An Ethnic Group

All members of an ethnic group possess certain attributes, which relate to culture, psychological traits, and ethnic consciousness. Ethnic group are endowed with distinct but achronistic attributes. On the one hand ethnic groups are stable communities, their basic culture components remaining unaltered over a long period of time. At the same time ethnic groups are dynamic, changing systems. This dialectical negation of one characteristic by another can be properly understood if it is remembered that even when one ethnic group is transformed into another ethnic group through the various ethnic processes its predominant traditional properties are preserved, though in a greatly modified form. The groups-specific cultural attributes include spoken language, religion, folklore, folk customs, rites and ceremonies, standards of behavior including courtesy greetings, food, dress and hygienic habits, aesthetic ideals and artistic culture, type of house construction, and others. No single cultural component, however, may be regarded as an indispensible ethno-differentiating attribute. It is the whole complex of these attributes that characterize an ethnic community in a narrow sense. However for the simplistic understanding of the essential attributes of an ethnic group some of them are briefly discussed below:

1. Ethnic consciousness is one of the indispensable ethnic attributes. This consciousness manifests itself in the common name-ethnonym. Other people may give the same ethnic community different name or names. In such a case the name given to itself by an ethnic community for self-identification is its ethnonym self-identification or endoethnonym while the name given to it by others is its exoethnonym. An endoethnonym has one meaning, and is quite stable. Exoethnonyms, on the other hand, originate under different circumstances, and may vary from one community to another. Nevertheless, some of the exoethnonyms have a deep historical significance as in the case of 'German', 'Manipuri', 'Jaintia' and several others and if otherwise found inoffensive to the concerned ethnic group, have a tendency to be used along with the corresponding endoethnonyms. For instance, Lushai is an exoethnonym that is used along with the corresponding endoethnonym Mizo, and similarly Manipuri is an exoethnonym that is used along with the corresponding endoethnonym Meithei. Another component of ethnic consciousness is the belief in a common origin, often mythical. Such belief may also take the form of shared memory of past migrations such as folk tradition of migrations among Garos, Khasis, Jaintias, Tiwas, various Naga tribes and others.
2. Ethnocentrism was introduced to the social sciences by the American sociologist William G. Sumner, who defined it in his *Folkways* (1906) as putting the values and norms of the own culture central in the judgment of others. Implicitly, this also meant that one's own culture is held as superior to all others. The concept was integrated into mainstream social science as a consequence of the classic study on *The Authoritarian Personality* (1950) by T.W. Adorno and his colleagues. Since then ethnocentrism has gotten a second meaning, that is, an ethnic or cultural interpretation of the more general process of "in group-out group

differentiation." Ethnocentrism combines a positive attitude toward one's own ethnic/cultural group (the in- group) with a negative attitude toward the other ethnic/cultural groups (the out-group). These interlinked attitudes are the result of two mechanisms: social identification and social counter identification.

3. The operationalisation of the positive identification with the in-group comes close to certain definitions of nationalism; that is, stressing national pride, the importance of national symbols, and so on. Some scholars consider ethnocentrism and nationalism to be inseparable, whereas others argue that nationalism, and chauvinism are just forms of ethno-centrism. The negative identification toward the out-group(s), on the other hand, resembles phenomena generally termed as prejudice, stereotyping, or xenophobia. In fact, ethnocentrism is often used interchangeably with these terms; some authors define ethnocentrism as collective xenophobia. Most scholars believe that ethnocentrism is a universal phenomenon. However, other scholars, mainly those working within the socio-psychological research tradition, consider ethnocentrism to be either a character feature of certain individuals or a product of a specific socialization process (within the family or within the larger society). They point to the strong correlations between high levels of ethnocentrism and low levels of education and income found in empirical studies throughout the world.
4. A shared memory is another essential attribute of the ethnic groups. According to Anthony D Smith, shared memories attach themselves to specific places and definite territories. The process by which certain lands of shared memories are attached to particular territories so that the former become ethnic landscapes (or ethnoscapes) and the latter become historic homelands, is called by Smith, *'territorialisation of memory'*. This is a process that is found in many countries and periods. It is often associated with sacred sites: mountains like Kanchenjunga in Darjeeling and the Nanda Devi Mount in Uttaranchal which is worshipped as a Goddess; sacred rivers such as the Ganges and the Nile; or special shrines like Mecca-sites and Amarnath shrine in Jammu and Kashmir that have attracted awe and veneration from large numbers of people; various tombs and monuments which mark the exploits and resting-places of heroes, sages, artists and statesmen honoured by the community. But the most important of the sites of territorialized memory are the various fields of battle that marked critical turning points in the fortunes of the community.

5. While factors like diplomacy, inheritance, marriage alliances and conquest determined the boundaries of most states, the memories attached to turning-points and heroic figures become the ground for subsequent claims in popular memory. Since these were crucial for the development of the community; any subsequent demarcations of the historic homeland would have to include the sites and territories associated in popular consciousness with these events. This is what makes the province of Kosovo so important to present-day Serbs; Ulster to many Irish, Macedonia to many Greeks and Judea and Samaria to many Israelis, turning them into contested zones where rival ethnic title deeds have resulted in protracted conflicts. The boundaries of nations and national states may be determined by military, economic and political factors, but their significance is determined by the joys and sufferings associated with a particular ethnos- cape that the inhabitants derives from it.[7]
6. However according to sociologist Dipankar Gupta space really refers to the location of interaction and not to the pure geography. When vicarious spaces are recalled it is not exactly geography that is being remembered but the density of social interaction.[8] It is when a location gets culturalized that it becomes 'space', thereby making geography analytically peripheral. A nation-state, to Dipankar Gupta, is born out of popular participation, long-distance communication, and large-scale supra-local mobilizations along ideologies that transcend parochial boundaries. The geography that becomes sacralised territory of an ethnic group depends on precisely those locations from where activism of this sort has emerged. It is only after this fact that retrospectively territorial alignments are drawn. Geography then becomes sacralised. The manner in which the United States of America grew from its initial thirteen colonies is an example of this phenomenon. In India the clear lines of territory emerged only after Partition. Prior to that leader of the Indian national movement were willing to recognize secession and national self-determination. After Independence and the Partition into India and Pakistan, preaching secession became a crime and this measure won support from mainstream political opinion and activism in the country.
7. Popular participation is another attribute of an ethnic group that makes geography sacred because new solidarity that emerges among an enlarged conception of 'we' finds its actual expression

through political participation in a cultural space, or territory.[9] The participation in a common mission leading to popular sovereignty is therefore a necessary feature for an ethnic group to emerge as a nation-state. However, it would be incorrect to project any one kind of mission as being more authentic then others in the making of a nation-state. It could be to bring about a uniform language, or to affect a religious reform, or to overthrow a foreign power. Moreover, there could be different ways by which each of these missions is accomplished. For instance the French Revolution brought about French nationalism, the unification of Germany on the basis of language brought about the German nation, the fight against Japanese imperialism spurred Chinese nationalism, and the struggle against British colonialism and the emergence of Pakistan led to Indian nationalism. The missions in each of these were quite disparate but they were all common in the sense of popular participation and in the eventual sacralisation of geography as territory. What is important is that in all such cases the end result should be the popular sacralisation of territory. When space is thus culturised it becomes an unfailing indicator of social membership. The space that this participation enlivens and encultures becomes the sacralised territory of the nation-state.[10]

The significance of popular participation based on nation –state sentiment as an attribute of ethnic group is to be emphasized given the established point of view which sees the nation-state as a natural culmination of given and primordial 'ethnic' identities seen as near 'natural' ties of blood, dynasty, family, language and religion . In this scheme of reckoning, ethnic sentiments and communities have existed for centuries in terms of their '*ethnie*'.[11] *Ethnie* here stands for group origins, history, cultural solidarity and belief in its common destiny. The ethnic view of nation-states and nationalism however fails to take into account territory, the culture space of a nation-state, and participation. Instead the primordial attributes are seen as all important. The fact is, as Benedict Anderson has pointed out, the making of a nation cannot be easily regressed into primordial entities. The manner in which the English and French languages gradually gained precedence at the expense of the other spoken languages in both England and France is a pointer to this fact.[12] What the nation-state sentiment evidently does is that it creates an ethnic community where there was none. Nation-state sentiment however is an outcome of actual participation in a national project enlivening a given territory.[13]

Approaches to Ethnicity

With regard to ethnicity a large number of theoretical approaches have emerged over the years.

Primordialism

Primordialism emerged as the early enthusiasm with the birth of the newly decolonized nations after the Second World War began to ebb. Nation building encountered serious ethnic resistance from within in country after country. Scholars explained this phenomenon on the grounds that the decolonized states were new whereas ethnic, or communal animosities were old and, therefore, historically deeply rooted. Ethnic group(s) exhibited a stronger primordial bond which is a more powerful motivator of human conduct than the pull of civic ties being forged by the new states. This view found its most systematic exponent in Conner who argued that "man is a national," not rational, "animal", and at the core of nationalism lay the notion of "shared blood", or "shared ancestry".[14]

'Primordialism' as propounded by Clifford Geertz, Harold Isacs and Van dan Berghe view ethnicity as persistent, changeable and, involuntary kind of allegiance. It is primordial since it stems from being born into a particular religious community, speaking a particular language, or even a dialect of a language, and following particular social practices. Primordialism, as discussed by Geertz involves the following three distinct ideas:

1. **Apriority:** Primordial identities are 'given' that flows more from a sense of natural even spiritual affinity than from social interaction. They have large histories and no social source.
2. **Ineffability**: Primordial sentiments are 'ineffable', over-powering, and coercive. If an individual is a member of a group, he or she necessarily feels certain attachments to that group and its practices. To Geertz, the strength and type of bond may vary but how such a natural and un-derived phenomenon could vary cannot be analyzed.
3. **Affectivity**: Primordialism is essentially a question of emotion or affect. The concept has most often to do with feelings. Primordial identities are also qualitatively different from other kinds of identities (e.g. class identities).[15]

According to Geertz the risk to lose a definition as an autonomous person, either through absorption into a culturally undifferentiated mass or through domination by some other rival ethnic, racial, or linguistic community culminates into the drive for personal identity based on primordial ties. This drive often interacts with the demand for progress, for a rising standard of living, more effective political order, greater social justice and exercising influence among the nations and in world politics. The insistence on recognition of personal identity and the will to be modern and dynamic thus tend to encourage partition, irredentism, merger or a redrawing of the very limits of the states.[16]

Jordan B. Petersen premised primordialism on psychological theories about emotions. He built four models, based on four different kinds of emotions; first, fear as an emotion guides individuals in situations of security threats; second, hatred in conditions of historical grievances; third, resentment in settings of status discrepancies; and fourth, rage simply expresses a desire to "last out" due to accumulated emotions, but without a specific target. A prediction was thereby made with respect to how each emotion would work, and accordingly a test was devised in Eastern Europe. Peterson's accordingly argued that it was resentment born out of status reversals that explained most of the ethnic violence in twentieth-century Eastern Europe during periods of state collapse (during and after the First and Second World Wars, and at the end-game of communism). Hatred, fear, and rage although explained fewer cases of violence, but they were also present.[17]

Anthony D.Smith viewed primordalism per se to be untenable, since it fails to explain why human beings are so widely differentiated by ethnic origin and culture. It maintains silence on why particular ethnic communities emerge, change and dissolve, or why so many people chose to emigrate and assimilate to other *ethnies*. Nor can it explain why in some cases we witness a fierce xenophobic ethnic nationalism, and in others a more tolerant, multi-cultural national identity. 'Primordialism' has been further criticized by various scholars for not taking into account the malleability of ethnic identity, its overlapping with other kinds of social identity, and people's capacity to assume various identities in different situations. In view of frequent migration, colonization, and intermarriage, particularly in the modern world, the primodial view of ethnic communities as immemorial, discrete, persisting units appears to be undermined. [18]

Instrumentalism

The core idea of instrumentalism is that ethnicity is neither inherent in human nature nor intrinsically valuable. Rather ethnicity masks a deeper either economic or political interests and so is often deployed in multiethnic societies as it is useful for gaining political power or for drawing resources from the state. Ethnic conflicts are strategically organized by ethnic leaders who manipulate ethnicity for the sake of political power, or for extracting resources from the state. Instrumentalism therefore views ethnicity as a political resource. It suggests that the manipulation of ethnic symbols is vital for gaining the support of the masses and achieving political goals.[19] Instrumentalist like Cohen emphasized that ethnicity is essentially a political phenomenon wherein ethnic groups and ties are utilised for the attainment of individual and collective goals. According to Cohen, traditional customs are used only as idioms, and as mechanisms for political alignment. This is contrary to what one may call 'the glue theory of tribalism' which states that the colonial powers had acted as 'glue' in sticking together within the framework of new, artificially established, centralized states, some diverse 'tribal' groups. Once the glue was removed when the colonial powers withdrew, each package state began to disintegrate and to fall into its original parts.

Cohen agreed that the centralizing tendency of the colonial powers resulted into the creation of many new states. But, at the same time noted that when the British withdrew, bitter struggles broke out over new strategic positions of power: places of employment, taxation, funds for development, education, political position, and so on. As result of this intensified struggles many tribal groups mobilized their forces and searched for ways in which they could organize themselves politically so as to conduct their struggle more effectively. In the process of this mobilization a new emphasis was placed on parts of their traditional culture. This gave the impression that there was a return to tribal tradition and to tribal separatism when in fact tribalism in the contemporary situation was one type of political grouping within the framework of the new state.[20]

Paul Brass takes the 'instrumentalism' approach further, suggesting that inequality between different ethnic groups or culturally distinct regions does not by itself spur the development of communal or national consciousness. Political elites at times even cooperate with external authorities and adopt the language and culture of the dominant ethnic group in order to maintain or enhance their own power. This kind of co-operation between internal elites and external authorities usually leads to a situation of persistent ethnic differences among the mass of the people, but without articulation of ethnic demands. Ethnic self consciousness, ethnically based demands and ethnic conflict can occur only if there is some conflict either between indigenous and external elites and authorities or between indigenous elites.[21]

Rationalist approach is another version of instrumentalism which emphasizes that man is a choice-making creature motivated by his socio-economic interests and his desire for survival rather than primordial drives. In contrast to the primodialist view that ethnic identity is given, it holds that people choose their ethnicity. For instance a Jamaican who is a citizen of Jamaica and a permanent resident of the United States chooses to be a member of an ethnic group – the blacks in U.S. and not as a member of the elite and demographically dominant majority in Jamaica which constitutes 95% of the total population. He thus chooses his ethnic identity in a real and meaningful sense that most befits his socio-economic interest. Therefore, the rationalists maintain that there is nothing permanent, unchanging, or primordial about ethnicity. The individual in fact is free to choose his context as well as the symbols he wants to make meaningful, i.e., whether to align with their ethnic kin or their class, religious, or gender identities.[22] In similar lines the post modern perspective of the instrumentalist approach holds that ethnic communities are simply cultural artifacts, constructs of elites who tailor pre-existing mythologies, symbols and history for their ends.

Instrumentalist approach, however, has been criticized by Anthony D. Smith to be seriously flawed. According to Smith it tends to exaggerate the ability of elites to manipulate the masses and fails to explain why millions of people may be prepared to die for cultural artifact. The intensity and unpredictability of the ethnic conflicts is overlooked by the instrumentalist approach. Moreover it fails to address why some *ethnies* are so durable and persistent, and why the masses readily respond to the call of ethnic origin and culture.[23] Walker Conner also criticizing the instrumentalist approach opined that although rational it has failed to reflect the emotional depth of national identity. He opines that nationalism and patriotism are two distinct loyalties: the former refers to one's national group; the later to one's state (country) and its institutions. Nationalism customarily proves to be more powerful force than patriotism because of the psychological belief in the group's separate origin and evolution. This sense of unique descent in nearly all case will not, accord with factual history. Yet, it is not chronological or factual history that is the key to the nation, but sentient or felt history. It is not what is but what people perceive as is which influences attitudes and behaviour. Both the frequency and the record of success of most political leaders who appealed to the sense of shared blood while seeking popular support attest to the fact that national bond is subconscious and emotional rather than conscious and rational in its importation.[24]

Constructivism

The central idea of constructivism is that modernity transformed the way mass identities were perceived in pre modern times which was largely locally or regionally based. Ethnic identities are constructed by bringing the masses into a vastly expanded framework of consciousness and meanings in the modern era. Constructivism identifies three kinds of mechanisms through which this came about—technological, ideational, and in the former colonies, colonial policies, institutions, and practices. The rise of "print capitalism" marked by the arrival of the printing press and capitalism is the basic mechanism through which local identities were transformed into larger national identities as pointed by Anderson's *Imagined Communities* (1983). The second mechanism that constructivists put forward is based on the arguments made by Taylor about how modernity brought about ideational changes in human life. In pre- modern times, one's identity was determined by one's place in the traditional social structure. People accepted ascriptive social hierarchies, or their "stations" in life. In modern times, hierarchies do exist, but ascriptive hierarchies are not easily accepted. While in pre-modern times, the notion of honor was reserved only for a few that marked relations between people of different ranks. Modernity introduced the notion of dignity, to which all are entitled regardless of their rank. The pursuit of dignity is however dialogical and not monological. It means that it takes place in interaction with others. To Taylor our identity is partly shaped by recognition or its absence, often misrecognition of others. Accordingly a person or groups of people can suffer real damage, real distortion, if the people or societies around them mirrors back to them a confining, demeaning, or contemptible picture of themselves. Non-recognition or misrecognition can inflict harm that can be seen as a form of oppression which imprisons someone in a false, distorted and reduced mode of being. Much of ethnic or national assertion in the modern world is therefore about resisting such "confining, demeaning or contemptible" pictures that the dominant groups through colonial rulers and state bureaucracies have often relayed to the subordinate groups. It is thus a matter of dignity and not material self-interest.[25] Anthropologists Clifford Geertz's is generally regarded as one of the most prominent proponents of this approach who viewed ethnic nationalism as a direct outcome of state-building projects. According to Geertz, modernizing governments with their increasing revenue requirements need civil servants who can manage military and police operations, collect domestic taxes, maintain domestic order and transmit necessary skills through schools. Such civil servants gradually emerge as powerful intermediaries between their government and the ethnic groups they administer thereby developing autonomous interests as well as the skill necessary to mobilize ethnic nationalism. Ethnic separatism is thus viewed as a "disease" of the transition from tradition to modernity triggered by the anomie and rootlessness of modernization.[26]

Institutionalism

The core idea of institutionalism is that the structure of political institutions such as consociational or majoritarian polities, proportional representation or first past-the-post electoral systems, federal or unitary governments determine whether some multiethnic societies will have violence, and others, peace. Ethnic pluralism, it is argued, requires political institutions distinct from those that are suitable for ethnically undivided societies. This is because simply a mechanical transfer of institutional forms regardless of whether a society is marked by deep ethnic divisions can cause ethnic violence. This argument is premised to views of John Stuart Mill in the nineteenth century who claimed that common loyalty to a political center was a precondition for a democracy to function. However a multiethnic society was likely to have many loyalties, not one. Tutelage as such was necessary until a civic consciousness emerged towards a political center and not to an ethnic group. Only then can order be maintained and ethnic violence avoided. It also focused on the relationship between institutions and identity choice. It shows how institutions can transform the salience of identities. Posner for instance argued that since colonial times, Zambians have had two axes of identification: language and tribe. Zambia has four language groups and over six dozen tribes. Since independence, Zambia has also had two kinds of overarching institutions: multiparty rule and one-party rule. Under the former, Zambians embraced language as the basic political identity since they had to elect a constituency representative as well as the president. This meant that the political arena was national, and therefore the larger identification that is language made sense. While under the one-party rule they chose tribe as only the constituency representative was to be elected, not the president. The political arena was reduced to the constituency level, and thus the smaller identification that is tribe became more relevant.[27]

Developmental

The developmental approach developed during late 1970s and early 1980s mainly deal with ethnic political mobilization. Walker Corner, an early exponent of the developmental perspective, contended that modernization helped to sharpen ethnic identity and ethnic nationalist sentiments in four main ways; First, Extension of political and administrative reach of government into outlying ethnic 'homelands' that previously enjoyed substantial autonomy by virtue of material increases in social communication and mobilization, led to increase in cultural awareness exacerbating conflict between 'alien rule' and 'ethnic groups' desire to preserve their autonomous life styles. Second, improvements in communications and transportation further generated cultural awareness and ethnic consciousness among minorities by highlighting the cultural distinctions between members belonging to different groups as well as the cultural affinity among members belonging to the same group. Third, modernization by widely disseminating the 'message' of national self-determination played a key role in the formation and justification of militant ethnic autonomist consciousness and sentiment in many parts of the developed as well as developing world. Fourth, post-Second World War global political developments such as the onset of the Cold War and nuclear stalemate between the superpowers, has made it more unlikely that a military weak power would be annexed by a larger power. It consequently led many small ethnic groups to seriously consider the option of 'independence' which in turn raised ethnic autonomist consciousness and sentiments.[28] Thus the central argument of the developmental approach is that ethnic identity and consciousness forms 'the essential independent variable that leads to ethnic political assertiveness and militant separatism, regardless of the existence of inequality or dominance'. In other words, it argued that distinct ethnic communities prefer to be governed poorly by their ethnic brethren instead of wisely by aliens as they believe rule by aliens is degrading for the community.

Another dimension of the developmental approach is the uneven development view that ethnic nationalism is an outcome of uneven development. Industrialization when results in "cultural" division of labour in which ethnic groups are confined to subordinate positions in the labor market will fail to overcome the pressure of ethnic separatism. This is particularly likely in cases where a core region uses raw materials and labor from an ethnically distinct peripheral region in order to fuel its own economic development. These peripheral areas after its integration into an industrial economy failing to develop industrial enterprises will act as markets for industrial goods produced in the core. The populations of such regions as such will become proletarianized and therefore prone to revolt, particularly during periods of economic turmoil. The uneven development view thus predicts that ethnic separatism will occur in economically exploited regions. The view can be applied to explain ethnic separatism in Great Britain as well as Asian colonies.

Reactive Ethnicity Approach

Michael Hechter was the main advocate of the reactive ethnicity approach. Upon his study of the Celt minority in the United Kingdom, he argued that it was 'exploitation' that characterized the relationship between members of the dominant ethnic group and members of peripheral ethnic groups in advanced industrial states. Such exploitation finds expression in the 'cultural division of labour' whereby valued roles and resources are allocated to the members of the dominant ethnic group. This however creates resentment among the ethnic minority fuelling their ethnic consciousness. In view of increased infiltration into their areas by members of the dominant group, the stunted development of the ethnic homeland due to its treatment as an appendage of the national economy, and the destruction of the social fabric of the peripheral region caused by the economic exploitation, peripheral ethnic groups may politically mobilize themselves so as to launch an autonomy movement. Hechter although studied the Celts in the United Kingdom, his theory could be used to explain political and nationalist mobilization among peripheral ethnic minorities in many parts of the Third World. For instance to explain the Baluch autonomist movements in Pakistan and the various tribal movements in the India's northeast such as that of Nagas, Mizos and the Bodos.[29]

Resource Competition Approach

This approach to ethnic political mobilization throws light on the causes of large-scale ethnic identity formation and ethnic autonomy movements in developing societies. A key aspect of the resource competition perspective is the dynamics of intense elite interaction and competition behind the politicization of ethnicity. International political economists tried to explain the rise of ethnic secessionism and clamour for statehood by many ethnic communities by referring to global economic incentives provided to ethnic minorities in existing states to seek secession. This phenomenon is likely to be more pronounced in states like India that lack the capability and resources to cope with the pace of social mobilization and to satisfy the increased aspirations which mobilization creates. Accordingly, states like India are particularly vulnerable to intense competition and conflict between elites.[30] In the early years of the General Agreement on Tariffs and Trade (GATT), when trade barriers between countries were still high, it made economic sense for ethnic nations and regions to remain in a large state with its large market. But with the World Trade Organization (WTO) regime created in 1955 after the successful completion of the Uruguay Round providing for freer trade, small ethnic nations and smaller regions can hope to become both politically independent and economically viable. The single European market, for example, provided incentives for the Catalans in Spain, the Scots in Great Britain, and the Northern League in Italy to demand greater political autonomy.

Economist Gary Becker thus contended that due to the rapid growth in international trade in the post-Second World War period, the economic prosperity of states is no longer dependent on having a large domestic economy. On the contrary, in today's global free trading economy, small states enjoyed four distinct advantages. First, for reasons of economic efficiency and competition for markets, small states by concentrating on only a few products and services can specialize in niches that are too small for large states to fill. Second, small economies, being more homogeneous, can avoid internal clashes among special interests. Third, the goods and services hawked by small states tend to be less exposed to trade quotas and other tariff and non-tariff restrictions because their volume and amount is often not enough to affect producers in large countries. Fourth, smaller states are more likely to be accepted as members by economic blocs and alliances, such as the European Union, since the volume of their production would not pose a competitive threat to the other members.

Becker further argued that the economic success enjoyed by small states such as Hong Kong, Singapore, Monaco and Mauritius, has had a powerful 'demonstration effect' on ethnic communities and secessionist movements in many parts of the world: 'Many of these groups concluded that they can do better economically by becoming separate nations and concentrating on producing specialized goods and services for the world economy.' Becker's examples included the Czech Republic where (after its split from Slovakia) economic growth has been rapid, unemployment has been significantly lowered, and exports have been reoriented towards the western states. Becker concluded that rather than being a handicap, small state size can be advantageous in international economic competition today and the realization of this fact is at the root of the current popularity of ethnic secessionist movements.[31]

The British economist J.S.Furnivall expounded in the plural society approach that multi-ethnic states cannot remain both stable and democratic. To Furnivall, an essential feature of plural societies is unrestrained economic competition between ethnic groups who live in close proximity to but separately from each other. Since inter-group relations remain confined to the competitive market place, these states failed to develop a sense of common political identity and loyalty that could overcome the cultural and ethnic differences between the various groups. Contrarily, unrestrained economic competition generates competing ethnic groups, which in turn causes society to fragment. Furnivall believed that the only way plural societies could be held together is through the application of the external force of colonialism.[32]

By considering all these theoretical approaches it appears that ethnicity based autonomy movements all over the world are the outcome of diverse as well as complex factors. It has an emotional aspect that stems from the fact that man is not an isolated being. His birth associates him to a particular ethnic community to which his parents belong. As he grows he adopts the dialect, customs and traditions of his ethnic community. In the process he develops an emotional attachment to his ethnic community. This emotional aspect although difficult to elucidate in rational terms has often been source of many volatile ethnicity based autonomy movements in the history. However the rational aspect of the ethnic autonomy movement cannot be overlooked in view of resource competition among the elites. The emotional aspect of ethnicity has often been exploited by a section of elites to meet their own individual goal.

Meaning of Autonomy

The term Autonomy is derived from the Greek word 'autonomous', auto meaning "self"+*nomos* meaning "law". Autonomy thus means one who give oneself his/her own law. This concept also finds mention in moral and philosophical literature. Within these contexts, it refers to the capacity of a rational individual to make an informed, un-coerced decision. In politics, autonomy refers to one's own self-governance. A large number of political scientists over the years have attempted to explore the various dimensions of autonomy. S. B. Ray Chaudhury viewed autonomy as a contested concept as it has been used to separate as well as to bring people together. While Samir Kumar Das proposed to locate autonomy as a space that is sought to be created within the realm of the state's institutions and practices. According to him, autonomy demands occur when the aspirations of ethnic community remain unanswered. Ranabir Samaddar relates autonomy to rights. Autonomy has become emblem of group rights and minority rights. Democracy to him has to be redefined on the principles of autonomy, as it cannot proceed without autonomy. He thus views autonomy as integral to the process of democratization.[33]

Ethno-autonomy Movements: Causes and State Response

In the past few decades, a large number of ethnicity based autonomy movements has emerged all over the world. Such movements often challenge the state-drawn political boundaries. They construct their own national boundary that spreads along the ethnic boundary different from the accepted boundaries drawn out by the state. This perception of national boundary travels down the kinship and cultural route.[34] However poor economic development and resource competition have also contributed to the feelings of alienation among the ethnic minorities that seek out autonomy to address the same. For ethnic minorities located in peripheral regions, the cause of their endemic poverty and underdevelopment can be for the following reasons; first, that the group has failed to successfully integrate into the national socio-economic mainstream and take advantage of benefits thereby obtained; second, that the group homeland has been infiltrated by members of the dominant community and other ethnic groups thereby creating an exploitative cultural division of labour in which valued roles and resources are allocated mostly to the "outsiders"; and third, that group members have failed to successfully compete with the dominant outsiders for valued but scarce rewards and resources, such as access to education, health care and employment.

A further impetus to the feeling of alienation of the marginalized ethnic group is the perceived perception of being "misgoverned" by the political institutions of the state that either lack the capacity or are unwilling to effectively redress the main grievances of the group. The four specific aspects of misgovernment as perceived by the subordinate group that mostly leads to political mobilization are; first, that government is too remote, opaque and unaccountable; second, that government is deliberately deceitful and neglectful; third, that government is corrupt and nepotistic; and fourth, that government is inefficient and wasteful in the management and use of public funds for development purposes. These perceptions may, either collectively or in various combinations, convince members of marginalized, exploited and subordinate ethnic groups that the politico-administrative set-up as a whole has either at best done very little to solve the socio-economic ills confronting them or at worst been responsible for creating and preserving their marginalized, exploited and subordinate status.[35]

Many of the demands for the formation of new states emanated from a perceived neglect, or what has been termed "internal colonialism". The essence of this argument is that the relationship between the dominant social group in a region and the peripheral groups-particularly those living in an identifiable territorial entity-was characterized by exploitation. The dominant group that acquired advantages over peripheral groups in the period of state building then use this political-economic advantage to maintain and enhance its dominant position. Autonomy movements have further emerged in areas that have experienced a rapid growth in the educational opportunities of the lower middle classes, enhancing their aspirations and expectations. Such an argument is more cogent if the ethnic group is not dispersed territorially as it can then readily perceive greater economic and political gains with greater regional autonomy. Class deprivation is therefore seen as being integral with the issues of sustaining indigenous culture and right to self-determination of the ethnic communities.

The state response to the challenges posed by such ethnicity based autonomy movements has been in the form of; first, granting statehood or regional autonomy by signing special acts and agreements; second, devolution of power through the institution of local self governments like *panchayats* and municipalities, third, economic development initiatives through people's participation, fourth, campaign for cultural and ideological integration into state nationalism, and fifth, resorting to coercion as a measure to suppress 'rebel' voice.[36]

In the past few decades, autonomy movements have emerged as a common feature in the political scenario with a large number of ethnic groups asserting their ethnic identity. Such movements often challenge the state-drawn political boundaries. They construct their own national boundary that spreads along the ethnic boundary different from the accepted boundaries drawn out by the state. This perception of national boundary travels down the kinship and cultural route.[37] Ethnicity having emotional bases that bestows upon an ethnic group a sense of unique identity and pride in their distinctive culture, dialect and history has now assumed a politico-economic dimension. Ethnic minorities fear that the influence of the outside culture might weaken their own socio-cultural fabric and deprive them of their unique identity. Such insecurity particularly finds breeding ground when an ethnic group is in minority in a particular territorial region. It is the fear that the ethnic majority might gradually assimilate the ethnic minorities within its socio-cultural manifold that makes the later apprehensive of the former. On the other hand, the ethnic majority because of their numerical strength do not find it needful to bridge the cleft which is eventually formed between the two groups due to the lack of initiative from both the sides.

This rift between the two groups is further intensified as a result of resource competition. Both the groups struggle to establish their monopoly over the economic resources to bring about the socio-economic development of their respective ethnic group. However in most cases it is the ethnic majority which succeeds to establish its dominance over the economic resources by virtue of their numerical strength. This in turn causes frustration to the ethnic minorities who view the ethnic majorities as the sole cause of their socio-economic deprivation. Such a rift which is mainly economic in nature is more common in the Third World countries due to its limited economic output and multi-ethnic character. Its failure to accommodate the economic aspirations of all sections of its population often leads to the growth of autonomy demands.

The gap formed between the ethnic majority and ethnic minority is further widened by a section of people mainly consisting of political elites and the rising middle class. This section of people claims to be the lifesaver of the affected ethnic groups. Appealing to the unique ethnic identity of the group they make the members of their group to view the other as a threat to their distinct identity and as 'colonizers' prospering at the cost of the ethnic minorities. Once they gather the popular support of their ethnic community they launch an autonomy movement which is seen as a viable solution to gratify their politico-economic ambition. Amidst all this ethnicity only ends up becoming an instrument utilized to add fuel to the frustration of the ethnic minority that frequently catches fire in the entire region making the masses on both sides victims of violent movements and subsequent destruction. In the present age of Globalization and Human Rights individuals have largely become conscious of their rights. His rationale makes him see autonomy as a one stop solution to all his problems – social, economic and cultural. As a result, most ethnicity based autonomy movements around the globe have demanded autonomy for their distinctive ethnic community.

Notes

1. Orlando Patterson, 'what is ethnicity', Bulletin of the American Academy of Arts and Sciences, Vol. 27, No.8 (May, 1974), pp. 26.
2. Ashutosh Varshney, '*Ethnicity and Ethnic conflict*', in The Oxford Handbook of Comparative Politics , ed Carles Boix and Susan C. Stokes, July 2009, pp.277.
3. Richard Jenkins, Rethinking Ethnicity: Arguments and Explorations, Sage Publications, New Delhi, 2008, pp. 15-16.
4. The Idea of Culture, Terry Eagleton, Blackwell Publishers, Great Britain, 2000, pp.34.
5. John Hutchinson and Anthony D.Smith (Ed.), Ethnicity, Oxford University Press, New York 1996, pp. 4.
6. Ibid, pp.6-7.
7. See Anthony D.Smith, '*Culture, Community and Territory: The Politics of Ethnicity and Nationalism*', International Affairs (Royal Institute of International Affairs, 1994), Vol. 72, No. 3. (Jul.1996), pp. 445-458.
8. See Dipankar Gupta, Culture, Space and the Nation-State, Sage Publications, New Delhi, 2000, pp. 104.
9. Ibid, pp. 113.
10. Ibid, pp. 116.

11. Ibid, pp. 112.
12. Dipankar Gupta, Culture, Space and the Nation-State, op.cit.no.8, pp.113.
13. Ibid, pp. 116.
14. Ashutosh Varshney, '*Ethnicity and Ethnic conflict*', op.cit.no.2, pp. 280.
15. Jack Eller and Reed Coughlan, '*The Poverty of Primordalism*', Ethnicity, opcit. no. 5, pp.45-46.
16. Clifford Geertz, '*Primordial Ties*', Ethnicity, op cit.no. 5, pp.40-45.
17. Ashutosh Varshney, '*Ethnicity and Ethnic conflict*', op.cit.no.2, pp. 281.
18. Anthony D. Smith, '*Culture, Community and Territory: The Politics of Ethnicity and Nationalism*', op cit no. 7, pp.446.
19. John Hutchinson and Anthony D.Smith, '*Introduction*', Ethnicity, op cit.no. 5, pp. 8.
20. Abner Cohen, '*Ethnicity and politics*', Ethnicity, op cit.no. 5, pp.83-84.
21. Paul R.Brass, '*Ethnic Groups and Ethnic Identity for Mission*', Ethnicity, op cit. no. 5, pp.85-90.
22. Orlando Patterson, '*What is Ethnicity*', Bulletin of the American Academy of Arts & Sciences, op.cit.no.1, pp.26-27.
23. Anthony D. Smith, '*Culture, Community and Territory: The Politics of Ethnicity and Nationalism*', op cit no. 7, pp.446-447.
24. Walker Conner, '*Beyond reason: The Nature of Ethnonational Bond*', Ethnicity, op cit no. 5, pp.69-75.
25. Ashutosh Varshney, '*Ethnicity and Ethnic conflict*', op.cit.no.2, pp.285-286.
26. Ibid.
27. Ashutosh Varshney, '*Ethnicity and Ethnic conflict*', op.cit.no.2, pp. 289-290.
28. Urmila Phadnis and Rajat Ganguly, Ethnicity and Nation-Building in South Asia, Sage Publication, New Delhi, 2001, pp.40-42.
29. Urmila Phadnis and Rajat Ganguly, Ethnicity and Nation-Building in South Asia, op cit no.28, pp.42-43.
30. Ibid, pp.47-48.
31. Urmila Phadnis and Rajat Ganguly, Ethnicity and Nation-Building in South Asia, op cit no. 28, pp. 49-50.
32. Urmila Phadnis and Rajat Ganguly, Ethnicity and Nation-Building in South Asia, op cit no. 28, pp.43-44.
33. Shagun Sharma, '*Exploring the Different Meanings of Autonomy*', Mainstream, Volume. 46, No 25, June 8, 2008.
34. See Sanjay K. Roy, '*Conflicting Nations in North-East India*', Economic and Political Weekly, Volume. 40, No. 21, May 21, 2005.
35. See Sanjay K Roy, 'Conflicting Nations in North-East India', op.cit.no.34.
36. Ibid.,
37. See Sanjay K.Roy, 'Conflicting Nations in North-East India', op.cit.no.34.

Chapter - II

Cultural Diversity and Minority Rights: A Theoretical Study

Liberalism and Collective Community Rights

Liberalism viewed collective community rights as both theoretically incoherent and practically dangerous. To Liberalism, granting of collective community rights to specific communities breeds the danger of undermining the sense of shared civic identity that binds a liberal society intact as one. Such community rights would lead to the failure of a democracy as different communities would refrain from accommodating their cultural needs in consonance with other communities thereby undermining the spirit of unity. Liberalism in order to establish liberal equality therefore advocates equal citizenship rights and equal access to opportunities for all. It promotes the value of common undifferentiated citizenship status for all the cultures in a liberal state that would develop a shared civic identity instead of differentiated cultural identity. It recognises the value of only those ties that are freely chosen and thereby advocates the centrality of the 'right to exit' in a liberal state. The Liberal theory of Justice that long adopted a 'colour-blind' approach refused to recognize any difference between the groups in a bid to treat them all equally. This theory however was challenged with the upsurge of movements based on recognition, ethnic identity, language, and cultural membership in western and southeast democracies. Minority groups, each with their unique history aspire for greater recognition and accommodation of their cultural differences. They even seek to secede, if they form the view that their aspirations could not be met within the existing state. Western democracies are thus witnessing an emerging trend towards the greater recognition of minority rights, both for the national minorities as well as immigrants.[1] Some of the views expressed by the western scholars are discussed below:

Chandran Kukathas

According to Kukathas, doubts have been raised on the relevance of the liberal political thinking with modern societies experiencing 'ethnic revival' on the basis of cultural integration. Liberalism that foregoes communal interests is challenged by minorities making political demands on the ground of cultural integration. With the immigration on the rise, indigenous minorities not only demand improvement in their economic conditions but also protection of their cultural practices. It is thus viewed that Liberalism with its individualist outlook has failed to contain increasing group loyalty and cultural reassertion by the ethnic communities. Liberalism clearly undermined the relevance of these cultural ties to the individual and thereby ethnic communities. Suggestions have therefore been made by scholars to forego liberalism and give way to more coherent ways of theorizing.

Kukathas however argues in defense of liberalism. He emphasized that liberalism is not averse to the minorities concern. In fact the liberal values of individual rights and liberty is to restrict the power of majority over the minorities. Liberalism is not indifferent to the interests of communities and so there is no requirement to seek alternative to liberalism or jettison individualism. Rather the fundamental relevance of individual liberty and rights is to be reasserted questioning the idea of collective rights for the cultural minorities. Kukathas however does not deny the relevance of the groups for the individual. What he tries to establish is that one does not need to do away with liberalism or individual rights to do justice to the cultural groups.

Liberalism primacy to individual rights over group rights is subjected to communitarian critique like that of Van Dyke. It is criticized for neglecting the relevance of group in shaping the identity of an individual and influencing their conduct. It is in contrary to this communitarian critique that Kukathas defends Liberalism by emphasizing that Liberalism although subordinates groups rights to individual rights it does not view individual as atomistic and isolated being. It recognizes the relevance of the social collectivity in shaping the loyalty and a sense of identity of the individuals. It is however unwilling to premise the terms of political association on the fundamental moral claims attached to groups. This is because Liberal theory views groups as dynamic and changeable entities.

Kukathas as such endorses the view of Donald Horowitz that 'ethnic identity is not static; it changes with the environment.' Groups in response to political and institutional circumstances constantly form and dissolve themselves. The existence of the group or cultural communities is conditioned by political and legal institutions. They do not exist prior to the legal and political institutions that give shape to group or cultural communities. This argument stands in contrast to the view held by scholars like Anthony Smith who criticize Liberalism by insisting on the "naturalness" of ethnicity'. Kukathas rather supports the argument of Horowitz that the group identity is the result of interplay of various variables such as culture, boundaries, conflict, and the policy outcomes of conflict. That group boundary 'tend to shift with the political context' thereby giving ethnic identity a contextual character. For instance, cleavages within the Telugu population in the former Indian state of Madras was submerged until the formation of a separate Telugu-speaking state carved out of Madras that gave fillip to the emergence of Telugu subgroups as separate political entities. Similarly, colonialism in Asia and Africa brought about the amalgamation of several subgroups into many ethnic groups. Groups are thus products of environmental influences which include political institutions. Thus culture although important is not fundamental in the constitution of group identity. Legal rights in fact can be an important source of group identity. This was the case in the late 1960s in Assam when Bengali Muslims from Bangladesh readily adopted Assamese as their language to become eligible for the acquisition of land reserved for indigenous populace. Horowitz is therefore correct to observe that culture is relevant in the formation of ethnic groups, but it is not an ineluctable prerequisite for an identity to come into being.

The liberal theory attempts to provide solution to fundamental political questions by appealing to the interests of individuals than groups. This is simply because group interest takes shape according to historical circumstances or political institution both of which are neither fixed nor immutable. It is therefore not feasible to ground fundamental political questions on the perspective of the group or culture or community. This however does not imply that group interest does not matter. They do matter but only to the extent that they affect the well-being of the individual. Liberalism views groups or communities as mutable historical associations of individuals. Accordingly an individual might choose to be a part of the communities that entitles to legal rights not granted to others. Thus group can generate entitlements and so can entitlement generate groups. Liberalism does recognize the right of the groups to guard themselves from the intrusions of the outside world and to determine their own destiny. This is rightly so as Liberalism refrains from accepting historical priority as conferring on a community the right to continued existence.

According to Kukathas, cultural communities are not just mutable but that they are also not a homogeneous group. Cultural communities are marked by differences of interest as well as internal conflicts. Internal divisions within cultural communities are of two forms; first, divisions between subgroups within the larger community. These divisions between subgroups were subsided by group's leaders who minimized cultural differences, standardized language, and assimilated different interests to form a united association with political strength capable of opposing colonialism. These movements of assimilation although a success could not completely dissolve subgroup identities that started asserting themselves with the abolition of colonialism thereby becoming a source of persistent subgroup conflicts; second, divisions between elites and masses is another important conflict of interest within ethnic cultural communities. This is mainly the outcome of modernization that shaped the distinctive interests of the elites. These interests involve good jobs, urban amenities, and access to schools, travel, and prestige. Elites in order to fulfill these interests seek political power. This in turn, requires the elites to invariably mix with the educated elites from other minorities and from the dominant society. This results into the conflict of interest between the elites and the masses within the minority community seeking self-determination within the larger society and wishing to preserve their cultural integrity. While the elites forego the prospect of preserving cultural integrity forming coalitions with members of dominant communities in pursuit of their career aspirations; the masses on the other hand assert their cultural integrity as the primary goal.

Liberalism thus does not think in terms of cultural rights. This is more so because cultural groups are associations of individuals with conflicting interests. It is not an undifferentiated whole but consists of minorities within minorities. Liberal theory seeks to avoid creating permanent minorities and entrenching majorities within an ethnic community and so adopts the individualistic instead of group perspective. It takes into account the interests of the minority within a cultural community and so does not give precedence to the interests of the cultural community as a whole as perceived by the elites within it.

The individualist view of Liberalism is further criticized to be assimilationist that neglects the need of the minority cultures for special protection and is therefore destructive of it. Kukathas however in defense of liberalism asserts that the cultural minority's right to preserve their culture must emanate from the individual itself and not from the culture he belongs to. This means that an individual should not only have the freedom to associate or form communities and conduct his life in terms of that association but also to leave a community or association by the terms of which he or she no longer wishes to live. Liberalism thus views cultural community as a voluntary association of individuals. It is the individual's fundamental right to exercise freedom to live according to communal practices or to exit the cultural community that is of fundamental importance. It emphasises the voluntary nature of cultural communities and does not give to it any fundamental right. The community's authority is contingent upon the acquiescence of its members. It is the members of the community who are entitled to the inalienable right to renounce the membership of the community. Consequently a cultural community is likely to wither away if it lacks the support or commitment of its members towards the cultural norms.

To Kukathas, the liberal individualist standpoint attempts to balance between the claims of the individual and the interests of the community. It although recognizes the existence of cultural groups but refuses to view it as 'natural' association of individuals bounded together with historical ties. Rather it views cultural community as a voluntary association of individuals with certain acquired interest thereby giving them the right to exit a cultural group they no longer wish to associate themselves with. However the voluntary nature of the communities also gives a great deal of authority to the communities as it no longer imposes the requirement on communities to be communities of any particular kind. Moreover, if members of a cultural community desire to continue with the cultural norms then the outside community has no right to intervene to prevent those members acting within their rights.[2]

Michael Walzer

According to Michael Walzer, Pluralism was shadowed by the idea of 'one people one state' which was a long tradition of thought. It was only in late 18th and 19th century that the traditional assumption of homogeneity culminated into demands for separation and independence. Such demands was premised on two ideas; first, that free government was possible only under conditions of cultural unity, second, that free individuals would choose if they could to live with their own national or ethnic community with political sovereignty. These ideas took the shape of a new nationalist politics that demanded unification of people to bring about cultural homogeneity. Here he cites the example of Yugoslavia and Czechoslovakia which were products of the early nationalism based on politics of composition and not division though it involved breaking up of empires.

In recent times secession rather than unification appears to be the recurrent theme not only in the oldest states like France and Britain but also relatively newer states like Pakistan and Nigeria. Colonial as well as composite nation-state is not bereft of the challenges posed by nationalism. It is in this context that the principle of self-determination has defined the collective self in ways that reflect the actual diversity of mankind. The principle of self-determination however can be applied in multiple ways. It involves not only sovereignty but also such alternatives as decentralization, devolution and federalism. These mechanisms are completely compatible with self-determination and can be granted to national and ethnic groups to avoid disintegration. They effectively loosen the boundaries of a composite state to accommodate the political ambitions of various ethnic groups. Autonomy can thus be used as an alternative to independence or sovereignty. It is particularly suitable for groups who are not entirely distinct historical community but exhibit some of its characteristics and retain a strong territorial base. Self-government tends to produce homogeneous communities and is successful only within such communities (United States being an exception). In democracy where politics is free, politics follows nationality. In fact Pluralism in strict sense, i.e., one state, many people appears to be a reality only in tyrannical regimes.

American Exceptionalism

Pluralism in America was as a result of individual and familial migration and not conquest and dynastic alliance as in Old World. Its boundaries were not determined by war or diplomacy. Consequently its nationality and ethnicity never acquired a stable territorial base. It was immigration that shaped the character of its inhabitants. Immigration to America was purely voluntary where immigrants had no bond with the land on which they lived. The demand for secession grounded on the right to self-determination had no resonance for the Americans who came by choice and were not forced to stay. The United States was composed of several ethnicities that shared only the American citizenship without a common history or culture. They were united in political sense but remained Germans and Swedes, Poles, Jews, and Italians in terms of culture and ethnicity.

Under such circumstances, patriotism was seen as an emotion which could hold the Americans together. Accordingly in the late 19th and early 20th century attempts were made to intensify feelings of patriotism to constitute the immigrants as a single people. This led to the process of Americanization described as the creation of a new culture in the crucible of citizenship. They prevented divisiveness as witnessed in the Old World;

gradual assimilation of the immigrants to Anglo-American culture became both necessary and inevitable. The slogan from 'many, one' took a deeper meaning in this context. The attempt to create an Anglo-American culture broadly involved two processes: first, restraint on all further immigration; second, rapid 'Americanization' of the settled immigrants. The process of Americanization entailed cultural naturalization of the citizens not political. The immigrants readily acquiesce to cultural naturalization. This was more so in the area of language as the immigrants made no efforts to maintain their original language. English was and is acknowledged as the public language of the American republic. None of the immigrants attempted to make any other language the basis for regional autonomy or secession. The only demand that the immigrants made was to separate politics from nationality as it was separated from religion. It was thus a demand not ethnic pluralism and not national liberation or secession. United States is therefore, as Horace Kallen called it a 'nation of nationalities', i.e., a country composed of many peoples,

The practice of Pluralism

Pluralism focuses on the intrinsic value of human beings for historically and communally structured forms of life. It views human beings as the self-appointed guardians of a society of groups resting on cultural traditions. Any kind of regimentation or uniformity is alien to them. Pluralism thus seeks for the individuals the freedom to uphold group identification and flourish their ethnicity. It pictures state to be unsupported by the ideal of either unity or hegemony. It insists on a state that creates national unity without denying or repressing multiplicity.

Pluralism is based on the three important ideas; first, it defends ethnicity against cultural naturalization. It upholds the right of the new immigrants, as individuals, to form themselves into cultural communities and maintain their foreign ways. It insists on cultural permissiveness of the individuals; second, is the celebration of the ethnic identity. This involves celebrating diversity itself as well as the history and culture of a particular group. The particularity of the cultures and creeds is to be recognized and appreciated which they either choose or are born with even though after conquest or immigration, they have to be born again; third, ethnic assertiveness of the new immigrants. This involves creation of institution for the new immigrants, provide education and welfare service and enable them to gain control of resources. Ethnic groups are historical communities but functioning as voluntary association; they must make ethnicity a cause and persuade people to 'ethnicize' rather than Americanize themselves.

American Republic has not suffered from radical divisiveness, as in the European empires. It exhibits the compatibility of ethnic pluralism and existence of a unified republic. It defeats the views of Montesquieu and Rousseau that ethnic culture and religious belief are to be closely interwoven. Rather there is a sharp divorce of state and ethnicity. American republic relegates both ethnicity and religion to the private sphere of an individual. Americans are members of ethnic groups in their private life but an individualist in the matters of politics. State and society although constantly interact are formally distinct. While society is a collection of groups; the state is an organization of individual citizens. The American republic has been remarkably stable, and state power has grown steadily over time as not single ethnic community has captured the state and turned it into nation-state. In fact democratic politics has made different groups to form alliances and coalitions as all are recognized as equal citizens irrespective of their ethnicity. This fosters unity of individuals together with diversity of groups. Democratic participation based on common interest however brings all the ethnic groups together. The result thus has been a strong political order.

Toward Corporatism?

The American Republic sustained the communal life of all its citizens and provided services that earlier groups provided to their members. It sustained their communal life, preserved history, defended their rights, prevented discrimination, collected taxes and provided welfare services. The state welfare eroded private philanthropy provided by groups to their adherents. State did not deliberately penetrate into the sphere of community welfare and culture but it was the individual that turned to state instead to groups for various welfare services. This made it difficult for the groups to act on own.

However, demands are now being put forward that politics must follow ethnicity, recognizing and supporting communal structures if pluralism is to survive. It thus follows that; first, both collective as well as individual rights should be defended by the state; second, that the state should expand its official celebrations to accommodate the history of all the peoples that make up the American people; third, that tax money should also be distributed to the ethnic communities to enable them to finance bilingual and bicultural education, as well as group-oriented welfare services and fourth, ethnic groups be given representation rights with the state agencies. Ethnic groups, as well as individuals, should share directly in the benefits of state power.

These demand point to a corporatist world, where ethnic groups have some political standing and legal rights and no longer organize themselves like voluntary associations. Corporatist state however is possible where groups have fixed population with well-defined procedures for choosing representatives who would officially act on behalf of the group members. United States presents a different picture. Its population that is mainly composed of immigrants has no fixed population, character and territorial boundary. Corporatist arrangement suits a state with rigid communal dualism as in the cases of Flemings and Walloons in Belgium, Greeks and Turks in Cyprus, Christains and Muslims in Lebanon. Here people could strictly identify themselves with one community or the other. There is no way that the various groups or even the state can establish such rigid communal distinctions among the different identities in America sans coercion.

Ethnic groups however can be guaranteed representation rights without establishing rigid communal dualism, of a kind that even pluralism could not produce. This is possible through the introduction of quota system wherein a certain number of Blacks, Jews, Irish and Italian Catholics, and so on, serve any institution at any given time but with no political relationship to their groups. They would not be responsible agents; nor would they be bound to speak for the interests of their ethnic or religious fellows. They would represent simply by being black (Jewish, Irish) and being *there*. Groups for quota system will be those who are victims or heirs of victims and are believed would not be present at all in schools, professions, and businesses if not for the quota system. Besides, such candidates are to be selected and not elected. This is because this kind of representation depends on bureaucratic rather than political processes. The chief purpose of the selection by quota functions is to give opportunities to individuals, not a voice to groups. It serves to enhance the wealth of individuals, not necessarily the resources of the ethnic community.

State and Ethnicity

A state committed to the ideal of pluralism can only ensure that opportunities are available to its ethnic citizens. It however cannot guarantee the flourishing of the ethnic communities. This is because distributive justice only provides the framework within which ethnic groups can flourish but cannot help groups who are unwilling to help themselves. They cannot thus be saved from their Americanization. To summarize, the primary function of the state is to impart justice and in a pluralist state, ethnicity is simply one of the conditions to impart justice. The state can recognize the ethnic identity of the groups but cannot make it a ground for improving their standing as citizens. Ethnicity can be a source of identification for the individuals and give meaning to their lives but it has nothing to do with their standing as citizens. Many states are still experimenting with the concept of Pluralism which remains to be tested against the long-term historical and theoretical power of the nation-state.[3]

Arendt Lijphart

Arendt Lijphart puts forward the concept of consociational democracy as a solution to the problems of a plural society. Consociational democracy refers to a power-sharing democracy. It can be implemented in a plural society that is sharply divided along religious, ideological, linguistic, cultural, ethnic, or racial lines into virtually separate sub societies with their own political parties, interest groups, and media of communication. These sub societies are ethnic segments and, in particular, ethnic minorities.

Consociational democracy is based on the choice between self-determination and pre-determination of the constituent groups in the power-sharing system among which power will be shared. Self-determination here differs from the concept of 'national self-determination in two fundamental ways; first, 'national self-determination' denotes the idea that nations should have the right to form separate sovereign states. In contrast self-determination refers to a method or process that gives various rights to groups within the existing state—for instance, autonomy rather than sovereignty; second, self-determination allows ethnic groups to manifest themselves instead of deciding in advance on the identity of the groups. It means pre-determination of the groups that are to share power.

Lijphart refutes the argument forwarded by social scientists like John Stuart Mill and Kenneth A. Shepsle that peace and democracy in plural societies is an impossible task because successful democracy is assumed to require a minimum of homogeneity and consensus and so cannot be established in plural societies. According to Lijphart the probability of a successful democracy in plural societies is less than in homogeneous societies. But the possibility of successful democracy in a plural society cannot be absolutely rejected as there are numerous cases of plural societies where democracy has worked reasonably well. Moreover policy-makers also undertake special measures to strengthen the probability of successful democracy in plural societies. Peace and democracy is a possibility in a deeply divided plural society if instead of majority rule it is premised on consociational democracy.

Consociational democracy consists of mainly four basic principles of which there are two primary principles (grand coalition and segmental autonomy) and two supplementary or secondary principles (proportionality and minority veto). Each of the four principles is closely related to each other, and together entails deviations from the pure majority rule. These principles are broadly discussed as follows:

Grand Coalition

A grand coalition is an executive in which the political leaders of all significant segments of the plural society cooperate in a grand coalition to govern the country. It may take various institutional forms. Grand coalition can take the form of cabinet in a parliamentary system. While in presidential systems, it may be achieved by distributing the presidency and other high offices among the different segments. Grand coalition can be further strengthened by broadly constituted councils or committees with important coordinating and advisory functions. It thus ensures participation by the leaders of all significant segments in governing a plural society. The best examples of the grand coalition in its prototypal form are offered by Switzerland and Austria. The Federal Council of Switzerland is a seven-member federal executive body composed of members of the four main parties in proportion to their electoral strengths, .i.e., two Radicals, two Socialists, two Catholics, and one member of the Peasants' party.

Minority Veto

The minority veto is a weapon that ensures protection to the vital interest of the minorities in a plural society. Participation in a grand coalition does not offer absolute protection to the minorities who may be overruled or out-voted by the majority on issues of minority concern. Decisions in grand coalitions are reached by majority vote. Therefore when a minority's vital interests are at stake, the veto provides essential protection. A minority veto thus supplements the grand coalition principle. It gives each segment a complete guarantee of political protection by enabling them to take decisions that affect their vital interests.

Proportionality

Proportionality is a principle of political representation that guarantees fair representation of minority segments in civil service appointments, and allocation of public funds. Like the mutual veto, proportionality is closely interconnected with the grand coalition principle. It serves two important functions. First, it is a method of allocating civil service appointments and scarce financial resources in the form of government subsidies among the different segments. It is a significant deviation from unrestrained majority rule; second, as a neutral and impartial principle it relates to the decision-making process itself. Jurg Steiner defines the proportional model as one in which 'all groups influence a decision in proportion to their numerical strength. It thus removes a large number of potentially divisive problems from the decision-making process and thus lightens the burdens of consociational government.

Segmental Autonomy and Federalism

Segmental autonomy is the final deviation from majority rule. It entails rule by the minority over itself in the area of the minority's exclusive concern. While decision making on matters of common interest is arrived by all the segments together with proportional degree of influence, its execution is the sole jurisdiction of the separate segments. It thus involves delegation of rule- making and rule- application powers to the segments in addition to proportional representation. Segmental autonomy as such enhances the plurality of the plural societies. It recognises the segmental cleavages and does not abolish or weaken it so as to establish a stable democracy. Federalism is a special form of segmental autonomy which has a significant parallel with consociational theory as it guarantees autonomy to constituent parts of the state. It involves delegation of governmental and administrative responsibility to territorially concentrated as well as non-territorial segments especially in the realm of cultural affairs. Netherlands, Austria, and Belgium are examples where the practise of segmental autonomy is extensive.

To Lijphart consociational democracy does not connote to one specific set of rules and institution. Rather it is a general type of democracy in which all the four principles mentioned above can be applied in various ways. For instance, the principle of grand coalition can be set up as a cabinet in a parliamentary system, as a coalitional arrangement of a president and other office-holders found in a presidential system or as in Switzerland in the form of a seven-member federal executive premised on a hybrid of parliamentary and presidential principles. Segmental autonomy may take the form of territorial federalism or of autonomy for segments not defined in geographical terms. Proportional results in elections can be achieved by the various systems of formal proportional representation. While minority veto can be exercised as either an absolute or a suspensive veto being applied either to all decisions or to only certain specified kinds of decisions regulating matters of culture and education. These four principles can be laid down as the fundamental rules or laws of power-sharing in a formal document such as constitutions or can be merely informal and unwritten agreements and understandings among the leaders of the segments.

According to Lijphart the consociational principle can form the basis of self-determination as a grand coalition can require the cabinet to be composed of all parties of a specified minimum size in parliament. This would make the cabinet an inter-segmental grand coalition of segmental parties. The proportional allocation of public service jobs and public funds can be organised on the basis of the relative strengths that several segments demonstrate in the Proportional Representation elections. And a veto can be given to any group of legislators above a certain specified percentage instead of granting a minority veto to all pre-determined segments. Segmental autonomy can be extended to any cultural group that demands internal autonomy through the establishment of a 'cultural council,' which is a publicly recognized body equivalent to a state in a federation. It is further emphasized by Lijphart that this kind of non-territorial self-determined segmental autonomy can either be an alternative or an addition to geographically-based federalism. That two are eminently compatible.[4]

Allen Buchanan

Allen Buchanan puts forward the Self-Determination or the normative nationalist principle which states that every 'people' is entitled to its own state. He attempts to establish a moral right to secede asserting that political and cultural (ethnic) boundaries must coincide. He explains 'people' as a distinct ethnic group, the identifying marks of which are a common language, shared traditions, and a common culture. According to Buchanan, a common objection to the normative nationalist principle of Self-Determination is the instability and economic loss that repeated fragmentation cost. However it the structure of world in which the potential nations live that raises serious obstacle to their right of Self-Determination. This is because most nations live not in compact territorial units but intermixed with each other in complex patterns. A territorial political unit can only become ethnically homogeneous, if it either expels, or assimilates all non-nationals.

Moreover granting a right of self-determination to all 'peoples' is considered unacceptable, on the implication that self-determination means complete political independence, that is, full sovereignty. Focusing on this implication, Allen Buchanan asserts that the notion of self-determination is ambiguous. This is because there are numerous forms and a range of degrees of political independence that a 'people' might attain and not just full sovereignty. For example, under some conditions, a group might consider itself to have achieved its goal of self-determination if it secured right to use its own language as an official language of the state, or if its territory was recognized as a province or state within a federation, or if the group's representatives were accorded a veto over constitutional changes or over important areas of federal legislation. Accordingly 'Self-determination' does not necessarily mean full sovereignty, and to recognize a right of self-determination does not itself commit to affirming that every group to which the principle of self-determination applies has a right to secede.

Allen Buchanan points outs certain conditions in which a greater degree of self-determination may be the only practical way for the group to protect itself from (a) destruction of its culture, (b) literal genocide, or (c) various injustices falling under the general heading of ethnic discrimination, including violations of civil and political rights that ought to be guaranteed to all citizens regardless of ethnicity, as well as discriminatory redistribution. These conditions are as follows:

Preservation of Cultures

The idea that the need to preserve a culture justifies secession is based on the belief of the members of a culture that their culture is threatened with disintegration, their very identities are imperiled and that in losing their culture they will in some sense lose themselves, or a significant part of the selves they value most. However various conditions, to Buchanan, is to be satisfied if cultural preservation is to succeed in justifying secession as a matter of right. First, they must show that no other group or state has a valid claim to it; second, the culture in question must in fact be imperiled; third, less disruptive ways of preserving the culture (e.g., special minority group rights within the existing state) must be unavailable or inadequate; fourth, the culture in question must meet minimal standards of justice (unlike Nazi culture or the culture of the Khmer Rouge); fifth, the seceding cultural group must not be seeking independence in order to establish an illiberal state, that is, one which fails to uphold basic individual civil and political rights, and from which free exit is denied; sixth, neither the state nor any third party can have a valid claim to the seceding territory.

Self-Defense

'Defense' here implies an effort to protect against a deadly attack by an aggressor. The condition under which Self-Defense justifies secession is in which a group wishes to secede from a state in order to protect its members from extermination by that state itself. Under such condition the group may either attempt to overthrow the government, that is, to engage in revolution; or may secede in order to organize a defensive territory, forcibly appropriating the needed territory from the aggressor, creating the political and military machinery required for its survival, and seeking recognition and aid from other sovereign states or international bodies. The restrictions on the right to secession on the grounds of Self Defense are first, only that degree of force which is necessary to avert the threat is used; and second, that the attack against which one defends oneself not be provoked by one's own actions. If such restrictions are acknowledged, the assertion that there is a right of self-defense is highly plausible.

Rectifying Past Injustices

Past Injustice here refers to the act of unjust incorporation of a community's territory which may have occurred in either of two ways: The seceding area may have been directly annexed by the currently existing state, or it may have been unjustly acquired by some earlier state that is the ancestor of the currently existing state. The right to secede, under these circumstances, is just the right to reclaim what is one's own, i.e., the re-appropriation by the legitimate owner of stolen property. The right to secede is thus a convincing argument for a moral right to secede in situation where the secessionists are the group that was wronged or who held legitimate title to the territory at the time of the unjust annexation, or at least are the indisputable descendants of those people. The restrictions on the right to secession on the grounds of rectifying past injustices is simply to avoid inconvenience or even catastrophe for oneself or others which accompanies secession.

Discriminatory Re-Distribution

A policy of discriminatory redistribution by government can contribute to the emergence of a group's sense that it is distinct and to its desire to form an independent state. It may lead the members of a group to construct a common identity in part out of the recognition that they are all victims of the same enemy. The process by which a group becomes a force striving for a state of its own is usually a complex one in which a political and literary elite forges a strong sense of identity by convincing people that the economic disadvantages they suffer are the result of ethnic discrimination, and continued discrimination may result into the disadvantaged group losing its ethnic distinctness. And when the members of a group perceive that they are barred from economic advancement available to others, the goods that membership in their distinct ethnic culture provides to them may become all the more important. This circumstance in turn may lead them to seek political autonomy in order to preserve their distinctive culture. Thus discriminatory re-distribution is a plausible argument for the moral right to secession.

Allen Buchanan thus provides various conditions that justify a moral right to secede. However he suggests that there are a number of measures, from special property laws, to minority language rights, to constitutional rights of nullification and group veto that can help to preserve minority cultures, without the radical step of secession. It is only when these alternatives are inadequate, or if the state refuses to utilize them, that the right to secession can be morally justified. Although whether or not a right to secede, rather than some combination of individual and other group rights, will best protect minorities has no general answer. It will depend upon the particular circumstances.[5]

Avishai Margalit And Joseph Raz

Avishai Margalit and Joseph Raz provide the moral justification for national self-determination. The idea of national self-determination to Margalit and Raz encompass not just a right to determine whether a certain territory shall become, or remain, a separate state or whether it should enjoy autonomy within a large state. The value of national self-government is the value of entrusting the general political power over a group and its members to the group. It grants the groups the power to determine the character of their social and economic environment, their fortunes, the course of their development, and the fortunes of their members by their own actions which are properly within the realm of political action.

Avishai Margalit and Joseph Raz put forward the following six characteristics which in combination qualifies a group for the right to self-determination:

1. The group has a common character and a pervasive culture that encompass many, varied and important aspects of life. They have pervasive cultures, and possess cultural traditions that display themselves in a whole range of areas which are of great importance for the well-being of individuals. Their identity is determined at least in part by their culture.
2. The members of the group growing up in a group must acquire the group culture. Given the pervasive nature of the culture of the groups their influence on its group members is profound and far-reaching. Their tastes, options, habits and patterns of lifestyle are to be marked by the group culture to a significant degree. Given that they are identified by a common culture, they should also share a history, for it is through a shared history that cultures develop and are transmitted. This tie between the individual and the collective is at the crux of the case for self-determination.

3. Membership in the group is a third characteristic which involves mutual recognition of one who belongs to such groups by other members of the groups as belonging to it. Membership in a group is a matter of informal acknowledgment of belonging by others generally, and by other members specifically.
4. The third feature leads to, and usually goes hand in hand with, the importance of membership for one's self-identification. Group membership is one of the primary facts by which people are identified. It provides primary clues for people generally in interpreting the conduct of others. Our perceptions of ourselves are in large measure determined by how we expect others to perceive us. It therefore follows that group membership is an important identifying feature for members of which are aware of their membership and typically regard it as an important clue in understanding who they are, in interpreting their actions and reactions, in understanding their tastes and their manner.
5. Group membership involves recognition by others as a member. This recognition is not conditional on meeting qualifications or proving oneself in order to belong to a group and to be accepted as a full member. One cannot choose to belong. One belongs because of who one is. One can come to belong to such groups by a slow process of changing oneself accordingly by adopting their culture, changing one's tastes and habits. Group membership is therefore a matter of belonging and not of accomplishment. It accordingly makes it suitable for their role as primary foci of identification. Identification is more secure, less liable to be threatened, if it does not depend on accomplishment.
6. The groups concerned are not small face-to-face groups. They are anonymous groups where mutual recognition is secured by the possession of general characteristics.

Avishai Margalit and Joseph Raz thus attempt to identify the features of groups which are important to the well-being of their members and thus explain the value of their right to self-determination. These features identify groups with pervasive cultures and focus on group membership which is relevant to one's self-identification. The groups exhibiting the six features are called by Margalit and Raz as '*encompassing groups*'. In it an individual finds a culture which shapes to a large degree their tastes and opportunities, provides self-identification and a sense of effortless belonging. Membership to '*encompassing groups*' is significant to its members for two reasons; first, since it is pervasive it largely affects the opportunities, pursuits and relationships marked by the culture and thus to individual well-being of its members. If a culture is persecuted, discriminated and denigrated, the options and opportunities open to its members will also shrink and their pursuit likely to fail; second, people's sense of their self- identity is intertwined with their sense of belonging to encompassing groups. Accordingly their self-respect is in turn premised on the esteem with which their groups are held. If their culture is not subjected to ridicule, hatred, discrimination or persecution the individual dignity and self-dignity of its members are maintained.

Margalit and Raz impose restrictions on the right to self-determination based on human well-being and possible human rights violation. Thus the right to self-determination is denied to perinicious groups so as to restrict them from pursuing repressive practices with impunity. Besides self-government cannot be granted on the ground of persecution because even neglect or ignorance or indifference to the prosperity of a minority group by the majority can cause suffering to the former. Such suffering can be dealt with other measures such as group rights and not necessarily self-determination. Lastly, interest of the non members is also to be considered before granting the right to self determination to a particular group.

To Margalit and Raz a person's well-being is bound up with his identity as a member of an encompassing group. An aspect of well being is an ability to express publicly one's identification with the group and to participate openly in its public culture. It thus has an important public dimension in the sense that public manifestations of group culture and group membership manifest individual well-being. Public manifestation involves respect for the group and its culture, and the absence of ridicule of the group, etc., in the public life of the society of which one is a member. Given the importance of membership to one's well being, it is vital that the dignity of the group be preserved. This requires expressing one's membership not only in the open public life of the community but also in political activities within the community. The political is an essential arena of community life, and consequently of individual well-being. Self-determination or self-government is therefore inherently valuable to provide the group with a political dimension.[6]

Jeremy Waldran

Jeremy Waldron is critical of the view that people cannot choose a conception of the good for themselves in isolation, but that they need a clear sense of an established range of options to choose from. He asserts that although choice takes place in a cultural context, among options that have culturally defined meanings, it does not follow that there must be one cultural framework in which each available option is assigned a meaning. Meaningful options may come to us as item or fragments from a variety of cultural sources. We need cultural meanings, but we do not need homogenous cultural framework. We need to understand our choices in the contexts in which they make sense, but we do not need any single context to structure all our choices. We need culture, but we do not need cultural integrity. Since none of us needs a homogenous cultural framework or the integrity of a particular set of meanings, none of us needs to be immersed in one of the small-scale communities.

To Waldron we live in a world formed by technology and trade; by economic, religious, and political imperialism and their offspring; by mass migration and the dispersion of cultural influences. In this context, to immerse one in the traditional cultural influences involves an artificial dislocation from what actually is going on in the world. That it is an artifice is evidenced by the fact that the immersion often requires special subsidization and extraordinary provision by those who live in the real world, where cultures and practices are not so sealed off from one another. Just as individuals need communal structures in order to develop and exercise the capacities that their rights protect, so minority communities need larger political and international structures to protect and to sustain the culture goods that they pursue. So in the modern world particular cultures and national communities have an obligation to recognize their dependence on the wider social, political, international, and civilizational structures that sustain them. They are not entitled to accept the benefits of its protection and subsidization and at the same time disparage and neglect the structures, institutions, and activities that make it possible for indigenous communities to secure the aid, toleration, and forbearance of the large numbers of other citizens and other small communities by which they are surrounded.

Waldron as such puts forward the cosmopolitan view of self. The cosmopolitan view does not deny the role of culture in the constitution of human life, but questions, first, the assumption that the social world divides up neatly into particular distinct cultures, one to every community, and second, the assumption that what everyone needs is just one of these entities—a single, coherent culture—to give shape and meaning to his life. The cosmopolitan view of self refuses to think of self as defined by his location or his ancestry or his citizenship or his language. The self is a creature of modernity, conscious of living in a mixed-up world and having a mixed-up self. It challenges the claims that are made by modern communitarians about the need people have for involvement in the substantive life of a particular community as a source of meaning, integrity, and character. Waldron uses 'community' in the sense of ethnic community: a particular people sharing a heritage of custom, ritual, and way of life that is in some real or imagined sense immemorial, being referred back to a shared history and shared provenance or homeland. Accordingly the cosmopolitan alternative undercuts the importance of the preservation of minority cultures. Cultures live and grow, change and sometimes wither away; they amalgamate with other cultures, or they adapt themselves to geographical or demographic necessity. When we live a cosmopolitan life, we draw our allegiances from here, there, and everywhere. Bits of cultures come into our lives from different sources. The self constituted under the auspices of a multiplicity of cultures has or can have a variety, a multiplicity of different and perhaps disparate communal allegiances. Waldron thus puts forward the vision of cosmopolitanism which provides the basis of an alternative way of thinking—one that embraces the aspects of modernity with which we all have to live and welcomes the diversity and mixture that it brings with it.

Jeremy Waldron thus argued that people although need cultural meanings, but that does not necessarily mean that people need to live within a single cultural framework. On the contrary, our cultures are a mix of many different elements which are taken freely from one another. In globalized world especially, we draw our allegiances from here, there and everywhere. Bits of cultures come into our lives from different sources. Accordingly the problem with cultural rights arguments to Waldron is that they try artificially to preserve cultures which live and grow, change and sometimes wither away or amalgate with other cultures. In the globalised world that we live today, people have myriad cultural attachments and cultural boundaries themselves are fluid.[7]

Seyla Benhabib

To Benhabib it is the institutions of deliberative model of democracy that offers the best prospect to deal with culturally diverse modern society in the modern world. This is because the theory of deliberative democracy is distinct as it beholds the vision of the interaction between liberal commitments to basic human, civil, and political rights, due process of law and democratic political struggles in civil society. A "two-track model" of deliberative democracy is put forwarded by Benhabib wherein cultural disputes are regulated directly and indirectly by the state, but without ending the "dialogue and contestation" that is a marked feature of the "civil public sphere essential for multicultural democratic polity". It is not sufficient to argue whether or not groups should have cultural rights when disputes arise over laws governing cultural minorities. Rather what is needed is a political process in which cultural minorities can put their case. Yet this also means that the minorities require recognizing that they themselves cannot simply demand to be left alone as their traditions are themselves often under pressure precisely because members of their own communities demand change. Cultural communities must themselves be willing to participate in the political process of democratic deliberation. To Benhabib, cultural communities cannot escape democratic deliberation since they are not fixed and homogeneous entities but bodies comprising different and contesting perspectives. The very boundaries of cultural communities are not permanently settled and are capable of being reconfigured in the deliberative process.

Benhabib rejects the two objections to the deliberative approach. The first objection is that the deliberative model is biased as it does not accommodate deep differences of belief and cultural practice. In demanding that consensus be sought, it in effect excludes many groups that will do poorly when consensus is sought. The second is that deliberative politics itself has limitations that cannot be overcome if it is to justice to the need for pluralist cultural power sharing arrangements and also to secessionist cultural and nationalist demands. For Benhabib, consensus is achievable; and group secession from public life has to be resisted. It is important not to overstate the significance of consensus, since it is at times important to defend claims made in the name of universal justice. As Habermas suggested that the "requirement of morality and those of compromise need not be mutually exclusive. Moral universalism and cultural difference might be in conflict, but the point is to resolve it through a democratic politics.

Western Approaches to Cultural Diversity: Limitations

Ethno-autonomy movements have been a common feature of South East Asia polity which stridently adopted homogenization policy post decolonization in order to consolidate feelings of oneness and to establish itself as a unitary state. Policies of assimilation no doubt met with resistance expressed vociferously by ethnic and religious minorities both through violent and non violent means. Any form of national homogenisation was condemned by ethnic minority groups that demanded recognition of their differences. Accordingly coming to terms with the irrevocable reality of their ethnic and religious cleavages government policies to accommodate minorities were adopted across the states. These policies however were mainly predicated on the Western models often unsuited to the specific historical, cultural, demographic, and geopolitical circumstances of the region with the legacies of colonialism and national liberation struggle

The theories dealing with cultural diversity and ethnic minority rights as enunciated in the western democracies although provides a systematic defense of minority rights has its limitations when applied to India having different historical background and circumstances. The rights given to the religious and cultural minorities in India was a product of political consensus reached after much debate and discussion in the Constituent Assembly. However the rights that were granted to specific minorities lacked a theoretical defense. The commitment of the Constitution to the welfare of the minorities was taken for granted as it was looked upon as a compensation meted out against them in the past. A theoretical justification as such was neither demanded nor given. The idea of group equality although received attention but was never theorized.[8] The result was a weak multicultural polity with no theoretical foundation that could systematically upheld the principle of unity in diversity in practical sense. Consequently the Multicultural framework of India has been challenged time and again by ethno cultural conflicts between groups as well as separatist movements. Moreover the fact that state mechanisms such as grant of huge economic funds, signing of peace accords with the agitating ethnic group and setting up of autonomous council have failed to provide a permanent solution to such conflicts makes the situation even more alarming.

To conclude in spite of the limitations of the Western Models in the West Bengal context the absence of any other well articulated theories or models of the democratic management of diversity makes the intellectual vacuum to be filled by Western models. This however may result into possible narrowing of the conception of the issues of cultural diversity. There is therefore an urgent need to articulate conceptions of cultural diversity that are more truly reflective of the circumstances in the region. The following chapters accordingly examine the ethno-identity based demands of the Koch Rajbangsi for a separate state of Kamtapur. The Koch Rajbangsi who do not share common culture, tradition and language with the dominant community of the state; the concept of 'we' and 'other' is clearly visible in their interrelationship with the dominant community. Accordingly their relationship with the dominant community as well as their rights as a minority groups is discussed with the insight provided by various theorists discussed above.

Notes

1. See Gurpreet Mahajan, The Multicultural Path: Issues of Diversity and Discrimination in Democracy, Sage Publications India, New Delhi, 2002.
2. See, Chandran Kukathas, '*Are There Any Cultural Rights*?' in Will Kymlicka (ed) The Rights of Minority Cultures, Oxford University Press, New York, 2009, pp. 228-252.
3. See Michael Walzer, 'Pluralism: A Political Perspective', in Will Kymlicka (ed) The Rights of Minority Cultures, Oxford University Press, New York, 2009, pp.139-154.
4. See Arend Lijphart, 'Self-Determination versus Pre-Determination of Ethnic Minorities in Power-Sharing Systems', in Will Kymlicka (ed) The Rights of Minority Cultures, Oxford University Press, New York, 2009, pp.275-286.
5. See Allen Buchanan, '*The Morality of Secession*', in Will Kymlicka (ed) The Rights of Minority Cultures, Oxford University Press, New York, 2009, pp. 350-373.
6. See Avishai Margalit and Joseph Raz, '*National Self-Determination*', in Will Kymlicka (ed) The Rights of Minority Cultures, Oxford University Press, New York, 2009, pp. 79-91.
7. See Jeremy Waldron, 'Minority Cultures and the Cosmopolitan Alternative', in Will Kymlicka (ed) The Rights of Minority Cultures, Oxford University Press, New York, 2009, pp. 93-114.
8. See Gurpreet Mahajan, The Multicultural Path: Issues of Diversity and Discrimination in Democracy, op.cit.no.1.

Chapter - III

Identity Formation of the Koch Rajbongshi

The identity of the Koch Rajbongshi as an ethnic community of India has never been questioned. Yet the trajectory of the identity formation of the Koch Rajbongshi in India lacks a uniform pattern. Consequential of the changing socio-economic structure of India the course of the identity formation of Koch Rajbongshi too underwent changes. The dynamics of the Koch Rajbongshi as an ethnic group was opportunistic of the socio-political changes that India witnessed during its transition from being a colony to a self governing sovereign state. This gave fluidity to the phenomenon of the identity formation of the Koch Rajbongshi which continues to vacillate and is lacking a well structured linear progress.

Traces of The Koch Rajbongshi in the Pre Colonial Period

The Rajbongshi constitute an autochthonous population in the north-eastern districts of Bengal including Rangpur (now in Bangladesh) and Goalpara district in Assam. They are indigenous community of the north-eastern districts of Bengal.[1] The history of the origin of the Koch Rajbongshi is largely based on the accounts by the colonial administrators and ethnographers. The historiographies provided by various colonial ethnographers provide a divergent view on the identity of the Koch Rajbongshi. An appraisal of their views provides an idea that the origin of the present Koch Rajbongshi community can be traced to the 10th century B.C., when they entered India from Tibet and settled on the banks of the Brahmaputra. They gradually spread over Assam and the whole of North and East Bengal. It is alleged that the Koches are of Mongoloid origin having close affinities with Bodo tribes like the Meches, Rabhas, Dhimals, Hajongs and Garos. But in course of time, they married the Dravidian and gave birth to a mixed Mongolo-Dravidian race having preponderant Mongoloid characters.

They assumed political power in the western Brahmaputra valley in the early 16th century, and exercised their sovereignty over the major part of the North-East. Following the invasion of the Kamta Kingdom, which comprised the western Brahmaputra valley, by Ala-ud-din Hussain Shah, the Sultan of Bengal (A.D. 1493-1510) in A.D. 1498, Biswa Singha, a Koch chief, organized his tribe. It was he who laid the foundation of Koch Kingdom in about A.D. 1515 on the ruins of the kingdom of Kamta. His son and successor Naranarayan (A.D 1540-1587) was viewed to be the greatest of the Koch kings, and an illustrious ruler of North-east India of his time. With the help of his brother Chilarai, who was also his general, he brought most of the neighbouring states under the Koch hegemony.

Following the death of Chilarai in A.D. 1576 the political hegemony the Koches held over the region shuddered as the kingdom suffered a division in A.D. 1581. The western division was known as Koch- Behar and the eastern division as Kamrup or Koch-Hajo. Despite this division and the political events of the subsequent period, the western division, i.e., Koch Behar continued its existence till its merger with independent India. While Koch-Hajo which preferred to play an inimical role against the great Mughals allying with the Afghans, was annexed to Mughal India in A.D. 1612. Koch-Hajo was later occupied by the Ahoms after the battle of Saraighat in A.D. 1669, and it continued to remain in their possession till the annexation of their kingdom by the British in A.D. 1826.[2]

Conflict on The Confluence of Koch- Rajbongshi Identity

There are diverse opinions with regard to the origin of the term 'Rajbongshi' as an appellation. Conflicting views by British ethnographers are expressed over whether the Koch-Rajbongshi is the same race or constitutes two different ethnic stocks. One is that the Koch king, Biswa Singha and many of his subjects, on becoming Hindu adopted the new name 'Rajbongshi 'or 'men of the royal race'—to denote their royal lineage. They adopted the appellation 'Rajbongshi' which was viewed to be honourable and dignified so as to validate their claim for the Kshatriya status. Francis Buchanan Hamilton's Report (1807- 9) for instance, stated that the Rajbongshi were the Koches who had adopted Hindu rituals and manners in the sixteenth century. The poorer sections of the community remained in the tribal fold and accepted a lower status in the Hindu social order. The affluent on the other hand, were elevated socially as Rajbongshi. Many of the poor Koches being denied the Hindu status ultimately adopted Islam. Thus a large number of the Koches became Muslims.[3]

Dr. Hunter too observed that, about the close of the 15th century one of the Koch kings Hajo (1510-1587) founded a kingdom in the west part of Kamrup. A divine ancestry for the Chief was manufactured by the Brahmins. Accordingly the Chief together with his officers and all people of the Kingdom converted to Hinduism. The converts abandoned the appellation Koch for 'Rajbongshi' as the new appellation to denote themselves. Hunter also noticed that in the districts of Rangpur, Jalpaiguri and Cooch Behar, the name Rajbongshi, which literally meant 'Royal Race' was adopted by the cultivators and affluent men and Koch being restricted to labourers and specially to the palanquin bearers. Hunter placed the Rajbongshi under 'semi- Hinduised aboriginals'.[4]

British ethnographer Rowny viewed Rajbongshi originally as Dravidian. According to Rowny, intermarriage between the Koch tribes and the Hindus led to adoption of Hindu rituals and manners by a section of the Koches who subsequently addressed themselves as Rajbongshi. He opined, "Intermarriage of Koch tribes with Hindus has considerably changed their old habits. They resemble the Bengali more than any other people. One class of this tribe, the Rajbongshi worship Hindu deities and have adopted Hindu manners" exercised by fiction in the mixing of caste… Now the great majority of Koch inhabitants of North Bengal invariably describe themselves as Rajbongshi or 'Bhanga Kshatrias'. They keep Brahmans, initiate Brahmanical ritual in their marriage ceremony and have begun to adopt Brahminical system of 'Gotras'. There is no historical foundation for the claim of Rajbongshi to be a provincial variety of Kshatriyas. The original nucleus of Rajbongshi was certainly Dravidian". Thus, British ethnographer Rowny viewed Rajbongshi as a part of the larger Dravidian tribe, i.e., Koch.

British administrator-ethnographers like Gait, Hutton, Dalton, Risley and Thompson were unanimous in their opinion that a section of Koch population of Northern Bengal adopted the appellation Rajbongshi from the early 19th century. It is assumed that modern Assam and a part of Bengal forming the old Kamrup were formerly ruled by many tribes like Danabs, Kirats, Asuras, Burmans, Chutias and Pals. They settled in the whole or part of Kamrup followed by the Ahoms, Khens and Koches. Initially these tribes were rivals indulging into battle of supremacy but gradually came closer through matrimonial and other alliances. The Ahoms occupied the eastern zone and the Koches started dominating the west zone of Kamrup. Gradually the Koches centred round Cooch Behar and Baikunthopur.

The ethnographers thus arrived at the conclusion that Koches abandoned their aboriginal culture and adopted Hinduism during the reign of the first

Koch King Biswa Singha who embraced Hinduism. Post conversation Biswa Singha named his kingdom Behar and the people as Rajbongshi. The Koches were thought to be of the Mongoloid origin but while speaking of the Rajbongshi in general an emphasis was seen to have been given on their being more an intermixture of the Dravidian and Mongoloid bloods. It was Herbert Risley, E.A. Gait and Dalton who among others believed that the Rajbongshi were of the Dravidian stock with an intermixture of the Mongoloid blood.[5]

Rajbongshi intelligentsia, political leaders and social reformers, however, strongly disagreed with the views expressed by the British ethnographers about the Koch Rajbongshi ethnic identity. They emphatically denied any affinity between Rajbongshi on the one hand and Koches, Paliyas and Bodo and the other.[6] The Rajbongshi scholars, like Haripada Adhikari and Upendra Nath Barman expressed their resentment against fabrication of the Hindu identity of the Rajbongshi by the colonial ethnographers. They also disagreed with the contention that the Rajbongshi had adopted Hinduism during the regime of Biswa Singha in the early sixteenth century. According to Rajbongshi intelligentsia the Rajbongshi were already Hindus and were recognized as *Vartya* or *Bhang* (fallen) Kshatriya.[7] It was the British ethnographers, who popularised the term Rajbongshi as Swaraj Basu asserts, "Nowhere at this stage can we find any reference to the Rajbongshi in the history of the locality. There was no mention of the Rajbongshi either in the Persian records, in the foreign accounts, in the Assam *Buranjis*, or in *Darang Raj Vamsabvali* (genealogical account of the Koch royal family). In this list there is no mention of the Rajbongshi, or the Paliyas or the Desis, though there is a reference to the origin of the Koches". [8] They viewed 'Rajbongshi' as a new name adopted by a racial group which had already been identified as 'Koch' by the British; and this rechristening was on the basis of a Sanskritisation movement for the purpose of reintroducing themselves as Kshatriya so as to upgrade themselves in the Hindu socio-religious hierarchy; [9] Diverse opinion is thus expressed with regard to the origin and identity of the Koch Rajbongshi.

Rajbongshi Movement For the Kshatriya Identity

The warrior-ruler model of the Kshatriya remained the popular and practicable model for social mobility and cultural assimilation for the lower castes and tribes in India. During the early phase of Kshatriyasation, the process was mainly confined to the tribal chiefs and kings. It was initiated by the Koch chiefs in order to strengthen their legitimization as Hindu *rajas* in their own society and to broaden the basis of their economic and political power. It was a calculated move on the part of the tribal nobility to improve their material interests through Kshatriyasation. Accordingly for political reasons the Koch Kings adopted Hinduism so to elevate to the status of Kshatriya. Subsequently, dominant sections of the Koches in the late 16th century abandoned their tribal practices and radically adopted the manners, customs of the Hindus. They adopted the appellation 'Rajbongshi' in order to distinguish themselves from the more plebeian brethren who continued with the appellation Koch. It was thus an attempt to be regarded as a separate caste and socially superior to the Koches.[10]

From 1872, the Rajbongshi of Bengal and parts of Assam demanded recognition as a distinct caste i.e. 'Rajbongshi' for a clear and concrete dissociation from the tribal Koches.[11] Consequently under the leadership of Rai Saheb Panchanan Barman the Rajbongshi organized the 'Kshatriya Andolan' or Kshatriyasation movement and claimed 'Kshatriyahood' for the social upliftment of the Rajbongshi community. The principal objective of the Kshatriya Movement was the promotion of the Rajbongshi from a lower to a higher berth in the Varna order and greater respectability in terms of the given conditions of the caste system in the region. Through Kshatriya Movement the Rajbongshi challenged the lower berth assigned to them in the Hindu caste system.[12] However the Rajbongshi of north-eastern Bengal claim for 'Kshatriyahood' was not a sudden demand. It was a manifestation of reaction to changing politico-socio situation in northern Bengal. There were many underlying reasons behind the movement of the Rajbongshi for Kshatriya status which can be broadly classified into social and political context of Kshatriya movement as discussed under:

Social Context of Kshatriya Movement By the Rajbongshis

The society in northern Bengal was structurally undifferentiated in terms of caste hierarchy and associated occupational specialization. There were no hierarchical arrangements amongst the autochthonous groups such as Meches, Rajbongshi, Rabhas, Koches and Garos inhabiting the region of North Bengal. Economically they were mostly peasants. The caste categories of the core Hindu society did not influence the social formation process of North Bengal. Accordingly, the social position enjoyed by the Rajbongshi which was numerically and economically dominant community was least challenged by the other indigenous communities of the region.[13]

However in the beginning of the 20th century the influx of a large number of caste–Hindu immigrants into the region from other parts of the country challenged the social status of the Rajbongshi. The immigrants with their strong awareness of casteism started interacting with the indigenous Rajbongshi in differential terms. The Rajbongshi were even denied entry into the temple. The Rajbongshi faced humiliation and objectionable identification from the upper caste Hindus. Nagendranath Basu in *World Encyclopaedia* in the early 20th century, mentioned the Rajbongshi as 'barbarians' and Bankim Chandra Chattopadhyay in *Bongo Darshan* mooted that the Koch identity cannot be synonymous with Bengali Hindu identity. The Koch- Rajbongshis were kept out of the Brahmanical fold of Hinduism in spite of their innumerable efforts to merge with the mainstream Hindu society. The Rajbongshi could not enter the Hindu fold successfully due to the resistance offered by the high caste Hindus. Consequently they remained in the periphery of the Hindu caste hierarchy.[14]

The incursion of the upper caste gentry into the north Bengal region changed the social milieu of the region wherein status dissonance was suffered by the Rajbongshi elites. The Hindu migrants to this region created resentment and anxiety among the local Rajbongshi as they were considered socially and culturally inferior and were accorded status of a low caste. This caused a section of the affluent and educated Rajbongshi conscious of their low position in the local caste hierarchy of the region. It provided them the impetus to make efforts for upward caste mobility and vie for the recognition as Kshatriyas. The leaders of the Kshatriya Movement were equal to the upper caste Hindus in matters of education, profession, and manners and felt quite acutely the odium of belonging to a low caste Hindu society due to their low social origin. The upper echelons (*Jotedars*, *Babus*, etc) of the Rajbongshi community demanded a corresponding high rank in the local social structure. They were the main advocates of Rajbongshi Kshatriya Movement in north Bengal.[15]

Subsequently the Rajbongshi became caste conscious, like any Hindu caste, and began to rank all the castes in their villages on the basis of occupation they followed.[16] Consequential of the land revenue system in the region over a long period of colonial rule in India the number of landowners in the Rajbongshi population increased. Effectively the claimants to the Rajbongshi-Kshatriya adage increased with an increase in the number of well-to-do landowners in the Rajbongshi population. The movement to get Kshatriya status was thus an expression of the aspiration of the landlords, *Jotedars* and well-off peasants. They were the main participants in the conferences and activities in connection with the movement.

Political Context of Kshatriya Movement By the Rajbongshis

The Revolt of 1857 did not change the colonial attitude though it changed their ways to rule. While a policy of non-intervention in the traditions, customs and conventions of their subject peoples was adopted, it necessitated, as Nicholas Dirks, commented, 'a new commitment to colonial knowledge about the subjects of its rule...[It] made the anthoropologization of colonial knowledge necessary for several reasons. Ethnographic knowledge could explain why the rebellion took place, how to avoid such disaffection in future, new ways to claim the loyalty of subjects on the basis of custom and culture, and how to delineate the autonomous and proper domains of religion and custom'. He further observed, "District level manuals and gazetteers began to devote whole chapters to the ethnography of caste and customs; imperial surveys made caste into a central object of investigation; and by the time of the first decennial Census of 1872, caste had become the primary subject of social classification and knowledge.[17] Moreover the upper caste Hindu community alienated both the Muslims and the lower castes from the nationalist movement in the colonial India. The nationalist leadership which was dominated by the Hindu upper caste elites did not have anything on their agenda for the well-being of the depressed classes. It was rather critical of the colonial protection for them and suspicious of their collaborative relation with the British. As a result the lower castes including the Rajbongshi were more loyal to the colonial authority for the protective discrimination.

In the Census Reports from 1872 to 1931 caste formed an important criterion to examine the claims of the different castes for higher ranks or more respectable positions. Census was thus used by caste groups as an instrument to improve their position in the social hierarchy by assuming new names or titles; and advancing claims to a position than that usually assigned to them in the social scale. The introduction of Decennial Census in the late nineteenth century in colonial India opened an opportunity to the Rajbongshi for obtaining recognition of their social claim as Kshatriya in the Census. They looked at the Census as a new government-sponsored channel of social mobility otherwise denied to them by persons of upper castes Hindus.[18]

The claim of the Rajbongshi to be enumerated as a Kshatriya but not a tribe (Koch) began to take the shape of a movement when the Census authority gave instruction to the effect that the 'Rajbongshi is same as Koch'. The struggle of the Rajbongshi for the identity as Kshatriya ensued. A recovery of the past and its glorification was considered to be prerequisite in identity or nationalist movements. Accordingly the Rajbongshi attempted to revive their past history to strengthen their claim for Kshatriyahood. The whole history of the Rajbongshi was projected to be the history of the Kshatriya kings in the regions of Pragjyotishpur, Kamrup and later Kamtapur and KamtaBehar. The Rajbongshi identity movement for Kshatriyahood attempted a recovery of the glorious past mainly to prove its claim to be different from that of the present status in the Hindu caste hierarchy.[19]

They pressed the British Government through persistent agitation that (i) the Rajbongshi be recorded separately from the Koch, and (ii) be recognized as a Kshatriya by descent.[20] In their desire to be recorded as a member of high caste, they passed through at least four distinct social identities from one census to another: Koch to Rajbongshi (1872), Rajbongshi to *Bratya/Bhanga* Kshatriya (1891), Bratya Kshatriya to Kshatriya Rajbongshi (1911 and 1921) and Kshatriya Rajbongshi to only Kshatriya (1931). The Rajbongshi presumed if they could succeed in getting themselves recorded as Kshatriya in the census, an official document of the Government, no one would indeed be able to dispute their rank in the caste hierarchy.[21] Thus with the onset of the census operations the whole situation assumed a new dimension. Those who were coming up from below looked to the Census Commissioner for public recognition of their higher status, for it would ensure reverence from the indigenous society.

The Rajbongshi set up their claim to be considered as Kshatriyas based on quotes from Hindu scripture and epics. They claimed that the Rajbongshi Hindus were Kshatriyas of Aryan origin against the census authority's assessment that Rajbongshi is same as Koch. Led by Harmohan Khajanchi several Rajbongshi Zamindars and Jotedars protested against Rajbongshi as recognised as Koch. Under the banner of "Rangpur Bratya Kshatriya Jatir Unnati Bidhayani Sabha", they urged F.M. Skyne, District Magistrate of Rangpur to recognize Rajbongshi as a separate caste and enumerate them as Kshatriyas in the Census. Mr. Skyne sought the opinion of the Rangpur Dharma Sabha, an association of Brahmin pundits. The Dharma Sabha after consulting the Brahmins of places like Nabadwip, Mithila, Kamrup, gave the opinion that the Rajbongshi were of Kshatriya origin, who have been degraded to a Bratya state due to non-observance of Vedic practices, and that Rajbongshi and Koches were two different castes. On the basis of this opinion Mr. Skyne recommended to the Census Superintendent to allow the Rajbongshi to be enumerated as Bratya Kshatriyas. He also issued a circular to the effect that the Rajbongshi could write their caste as Bratya Kshyatriyas in all official correspondence. This pacified the Rajbongshi and the Movement subsided. The movement, however, gathered momentum during the Census of 1901 when the Rajbongshi, found that they were retreated under the category of Koch, which was abhorred by the Rajbongshi. This generated considerable discontent and they urged the concerned authority to accord them the status of Kshatriya caste. Their claim was however, not acceded to because of opposition from sections of upper caste Hindus.[22]

Kshatriya Samiti

The Rajbongshi for institutional support to their endeavour to get recognized as Kshatriya and for mass mobilization constituted a caste-based association, called '*Kshatriya Samiti'* at Rangpur in 1910. It was formed with the initiative of an elite Rajbongshi group of Rangpur led by Rai Saheb Panchanan Barma, a lawyer and popularly known in his community as 'Thakur Panchanan'. The immediate objective of the Kshatriya Samiti was to exert pressure on the Census authorities to grant them Kshatriya status. The Kshatriya Samiti had some other objectives to fulfil too. It intended to separate the tribal Koch and the Rajbongshi identity emphasizing the superior status of the latter, to legitimize the demand to include the Rajbongshi within the Kshatriya caste and to indoctrinate Brahmanical values and practices among the Rajbongshi. The *Samiti* articulated as well as organised new initiative to mobility along the axis of status.

There were serious efforts on the part of the *Samiti* to secure the opinion of Brahman Priests of Nababwip and Banaras and other Vedic sanctions to validate their claim to Kshatriya identity. They wanted to legitimise the elevation of their ritual status into "Kshatriyas" by the priests and genealogists. With the help of the relevant clues from the Vedic literature and support of Brahmin Priests from Kashi, Nabadip, Methila, Kamrup, the Kshatriya Samiti cited the different code of laws which reinforced their Kshatriya origin. Mythology and traditions were also frequently cited in support of their claim to be recognized as descendents of Kshatriya Varna. Attempts were being made by a section of Rajbongshi intelligentsia to construct 'new' history of the Rajbongshi taking the materials from folk tales, folk songs, legends and proverbs to establish their claim.[23] The earliest attempt to write the history of the Rajbongshi community was made by Harikishore Adhikari who wrote *Rajbongshi Kulaprodip* in Bengali and published it from Calcutta in 1908. He based his writings on Hindu scriptures and attempted to prove that the Rajbongshi were Kshatriyas and descendents of a Royal lineage.

However it was Sri Panchanan Barman of the "Kshatriya Sabha", who suggested a historical link of the present Rajbongshi community with

Bhaskar Barman, king of Kamrupa (present Assam) in 7th century A.D. It was suggested that after the exit of Palas of Kamarupa in 12th century A.D, their capital Kamarupanagara might have grown into Kamtanagara during the reign of the Khens in the 15th Century. Husain Shah ousted Khens and assumed the title "Conqueror of Kamta". It was in the beginning of 16th Century that the Koch Chieftain Visvasimha drove away the Muslim intruders and established the Narayani dynasty with his capital at Kamtanagari. In course of time he consolidated his power over the entire western part of the region from river Karatoya to the Barnadi, after defeating the local Bhuyans of Assam. In 1562, a Koch army under the leadership of Narnarayana, the son of Visvasimha marched to the Ahom capital Garhgaon and annexed it. But soon the kingdom was split into two, Koch Behar and Koch Hajo. Koch Hajo was better known as Kamarupa, a part of modern Assam along the border of river Sankosha. The Kamta Koch kingdom continued to exist through the Anglo Koch treaty of 1773 down to its merger with the Indian union in 1949-50 by the Cooch Bihar Merger Agreement (Aug 28th, 1949).[24]

The Rajbongshi under the auspices of the Kshatriya Samiti boosted up their claim of pure Kshatriyahood. They began to emulate many Hindu manners and customs discarding their old practices in order to justify their Kshatriya appellation and Aryan origin. They typically attempted to improve their social standing by altering their customs to resemble the ways of life of the upper caste. They started wearing sacred thread and adopted *gotra* (clan) name. They also reduced the period of mourning and ritual pollution from thirty to twelve days to correspond with that of the Kshatriya. Discarding their original 'Das' title; many of them adopted Kshatriya surnames like Barma, Burman, Singh and Roy. As the struggle for Kshatriyahood became more insistent Rajbongshi started adopted practices associated with upper caste Hindus like marrying their daughters at an early age and keeping their women behind veil. Instead of availing ritual services from their traditional priests a section of Rajbongshi availed ritual services from the upper caste Hindu Brahmins.

The Kshatriya Samiti further launched a popular reform movement (*shuddhi*) for donning the sacred thread by all the Rajbongshi as an attempt to inculcate Brahmanical values. Since 1912, a number of mass thread wearing ceremonies (*Milan Kshetra*) were organized in different districts where Rajbongshi donned the sacred thread as a mark of Kshatriya. The Kshatriya Samiti made several attempts to sanskritise the style of life and cultural practices of Rajbongshi. The Samiti not only put forward the claim to higher social status but also urged their members to abandon the practices considered degrading by the upper castes such as the practices of informal connubial relations, polygamy, widow-remarriage and drinking of liquor.

In adjunct to above attempts to sanskritise their life ways, the leaders of the Rajbongshi Kshatriya movement felt the need of involvement in formal education and white collar jobs. They became aware that a new prestige system has emerged, in which, education, urban occupations, and a westernized style of life were important ingredients for higher social ranking and mobility. The Samiti however failed to create interest among the poor Rajbongshi on the issue of socio-cultural reforms. The activities of the Samiti became the monopoly of a handful of Rajbongshi literates and its conferences were mostly attended only by the upper section of the community. Nevertheless the Kshtriyasation movement organized by the Kshatriya Samiti was successful in the creation of identity consciousness mainly among the educated and well to do section of the Rajbongshi community.

Impact of Kshatriysation Movement on The Identity of Rajbongshis

The Kshatriya Movement was led by a group of Rajbongshi leaders who were the product of political, social and economic changes introduced by the colonial government in the nineteenth century. These Rajbongshi leaders, in their education, profession, and manners were similar to upper caste Hindu. They basically belonged to the landholding class and constituted the elite section of the Rajbongshi community. These ambitious Rajbongshi elites felt more strongly than their rural counterparts the odium of caste Hindu society due to their low social origin. The poor Rajbongshi were quite unaffected by the issue involved in Kshatriya movement and the emulative practices remained exclusive to the wealthy-upper section of the Rajbongshi community. Due to their financial inability to adopt upper caste's customs and rites, the poor Rajbongshi continued to follow their old distinctive practices. They also refrained from participating in the *Shuddhi* (purificatory) ceremony. For many of them it was simply beyond their means to perform the costly rituals involved in wearing sacred thread and they preferred to follow their old non-Sanskritic (non-Varna) rites and rituals. [25]

Thus the Kshatriya movement got a class character where poor Rajbongshi were less represented and less concerned to the issues involved. The Rajbongshi -Kshatriya mobility movement on the whole, remained confined to upper echelons of the Rajbongshi community who modelled their behaviour along the styles of life of the upper castes Hindu. The poor, on the other hand, were unable to fully identify themselves with the higher strata of the Rajbongshi society. Consequently on the issue of Kshatriya identity, divergent concerns of the Rajbongshi elites and subalterns came to the fore. The rural poor who constituted the bulk of Rajbongshi peasantry were unable to identify themselves fully with the people of the high strata of their community. Ultimately, observances or non-observances of sanskritised socio-ritual practices led to inter-class differentiation and social distance on the issue of Kshatriyasation within the Rajbongshi community. Differences between the elites and the subalterns continued during the Tebhanga Movement when the Rajbongshi *Adhiars* (share croppers) rose against the Rajbongshi *Jotedar* (landowners) to acquire their 2/3 share of the produce in spite of repeated appeals by the Kshatriya *Samiti*. The Kshatriya movement failed to crystallize a distinct 'social identity' for the Rajbongshi.[26]

The Kshatriya movement was not without its own structural contradictions and tensions. The off-short members of the community (*Polias*) who were considered as pseudo Rajbongshi by the leaders of the Kshatriya Movement denied from donning them sacred thread. They later got united and launched campaign against such discrimination. They gave a call to denounce the emulative customs and ritual practices followed by the Kshatriya brethren. In response to such a call, a number of Rajbongshi who donned the sacred thread discarded it. The structural differentiation within the Rajbongshi society became quite apparent. The community ultimately got segmented into three well defined endogamous sub-groups: the *upabits* (who retained sacred thread), the *pattits* (who donned sacred thread but discarded it later), and the a*nupabits* (who did not conform to change and were debarred from wearing sacred thread). There was no commensal relation among these newly emerged sub-groups. Kshatriyasation thus ultimately led to sharp social segmentation within the Rajbongshi community. It failed to play a meaningful role in achieving transformation of Rajbongshi identity as a whole.[27]

The upper caste Hindu was against any upper mobility of the Rajbongshi in terms of social hierarchy. The upper caste Hindu landlords and professionals strongly protested against the demand by the 'Rangpur Bratya Kshatriya Jatir Unnati Vidhayani Sabha' to adopt Bratya Kshatriya as their caste. In fact they put forward this protest to Mr. F.A. Skyne, the then District Magistrate of Rangpur. In spite of their attempt to Kshatriya mobility the Rajbongshi were not treated at par with the upper caste Hindus.

The Movement for 'Kshatriyasation' created much tensions and status-anxiety among the Rajbongshi with no benefits in concrete terms. The Rajbongshi did not receive any official recognition as Kshatriya. In 1911

Census, while the first demand to separate the tribal Koch and the Rajbongshi identity was conceded, the second one i.e. to include the Rajbongshi within the Kshatriya caste was turned down. All their efforts to get recognized as Kshatriya had ultimately failed except successfully enlisting their name as 'Rajbongshi' in the Census separately from the tribal Koches. Similarly, the princely family of Cooch Behar never encouraged its subjects to demand the same social status which was considered as its exclusive privilege. Thus the attempt to elevate their status while staying within the caste hierarchy failed whereby, the nature of social relationship between the Rajbongshi and the other "higher castes " and the rules specifying this relationship remained more or less unaltered.[28]

Protective Discrimination and Consequential Construction of Rajbongshi Social Identity

'Protective discrimination' was a persistent feature of British policy in Bengal. The British for their own colonial interest in India introduced a system of preferential treatment in favour of certain castes and communities. The imperialistic policy of protective discrimination sought to grant special favour in matters of education, employment and constitutional rights, first to the Muslims and then to the 'depressed classes'[29]. It was part of their strategy to curb anti-imperialist movement and to mobilize numerous 'depressed' castes in support of the British rule. Such a policy developed a separate identity among the Depressed Classes, later called the Scheduled Castes, because the ethnic and caste status of the individual was taken into consideration by the British government for extending official patronage. Different castes and communities developed a vested interest in maintaining a separate 'backward' identity. The policy of protective discrimination opened new frontier of social alienation and restructuration in Indian society.

The Rajbongshi also realized that a new prestige system had emerged, in which education, white collar occupations were important ingredients for social ranking and mobility. Therefore, they looked at the government for official patronage and in extending them preferential treatment in matters of education, employment and legislators. The Rajbongshi thus got caught in between ritual rank aspirations *via* Kshatriyasation at one point and the prospect of material achievement via protective discrimination on the other. The social movement of the Rajbongshi which initially began for achieving superior status in the caste hierarchy was thus ultimately reduced to a mere politics for reservation. In due course, that led to certain confusion, contradiction and change in social identity of the Rajbongshi.

The Kshatriya Samiti leaders had reservations about being classified as a Depressed Class because of the stigma of 'untouchability' attached to this particular social category. The Rajbongshi leaders, because of their claimed higher ritual status in the Varna order, were keen on demarcating themselves from 'Bengal Depressed Class Association' which represented the untouchable castes, and organized a separate forum called 'Bangiya Jana Sangh'. But later the Kshatriya Samiti was not in a position to cope with the pitiable socio-economic condition of the Rajbongshi masses.[30] The Samiti leaders, realized that by being included in the new legal category, they be branded as 'backward' or 'low' in the official caste category, but would certainly help in empowering the poor Rajbongshi educationally and occupationally. They conceded that merely attaining a high Varna (Kshatriya) would not help to improve the condition of those poor Rajbongshi who were economically vulnerable, and so they need special protection. Contradictions in the Kshatriya movement became apparent as the Samiti started praying to the British Government for special favours (protective treatment) in their uncertain position in the caste hierarchy and deplorable economic condition of the Rajbongshi masses.[31] The leaders of the Samiti at this stage were frantically seeking accommodation in the government sponsored institutional framework of protective discrimination. Accordingly, the Kshatriya Samiti started functioning as a political interest group having no objection to be recognized as a Scheduled Caste for availing preferential treatment.

Thus, addressing a conference of the Kshtriya Samiti held at Jalpaiguri on July 18th 1935, F.W. Robertson, the Divisional Commissioner of *Rajshahi* declared that the government had recognized the Rajbongshi as one of the Scheduled Castes, and that it would specially consider them for reservation in government services and also other matters of interest. Ultimately in 1936, the Rajbongshi of Bengal had got their place in the Scheduled Castes in Bengal and thus the Rajbongshi got a new identity as Scheduled Caste. The framers of Indian Constitution also adopted the term Scheduled Castes coined by the British. And after Independence, as per Article 341 of Indian Constitution and orders of 1950 and 1956, the Rajbongshi remained as Scheduled Castes in West Bengal.[32] The Rajbongshi is one of the 16 major Scheduled Castes of West Bengal. According to 2001 Census, the Rajbongshi comprised about 18.4 per cent of total Scheduled Caste population of West Bengal.[33] Thus the immediate effectuating impact of the scheme of protective discrimination was the formation of the Rajbongshi social identity as the Scheduled Caste of West Bengal.

Retraction to the Koch- Rajbongshi Identity

The Rajbongshi of West Bengal at present are striving for tribal status retracing to their old ethnic affinity with the tribal Koches. The major arguments which have been put forward behind such a demand are; first, it has been accepted by Rajbongshi intelligentsia that the Koch-Rajbongshi originally belongs to the Indo-Mongolian tribal stock; second, the Koch-Rajbongshi of Assam and Bengal cannot have two separate officially ascribed statuses.[34] While their kindred in West Bengal have been getting, some special benefits as a Scheduled Caste since 1936, the Koch-Rajbongshi in undivided Assam were declared OBC in 1953. They were further categorized as MOBC (More Other Backward Classes) in lower Assam (Goalpara district), while those in upper Assam districts were identified as simple OBC. In Meghalaya they were identified as a Scheduled Tribe, in Tripura as a Scheduled Caste, and recently in Bihar as a Backward Class (BC). Thus the offshoots of the same ethnic group achieved different status and identities for administrative purposes.[35] To the Rajbongshi such a differential treatment leads to confusion in their ethnic identity and affects social intercourse between the Rajbongshi living in two adjoining political units. Therefore, the Rajbongshi demand that no such differentiation in fixing statutory identity to the people belonging to the same ethnic stock should be allowed and; third, due to their ambiguous social position in the caste hierarchy and officially as ascriptive backward groups, the Koch-Rajbongshi suffer from various discriminations in socio-economic and political spheres. Therefore, a uniform ethnic identity and official status may help them in mitigating many problems from which the Rajbongshi community have been presently suffering.

Consequently the demand for conferring ST status to the Koch-Rajbongshi was mooted in an international conference of the community held at Bhadrapur in Eastern Nepal during March 9th-11th, 1996. Delegates from Bhutan, Bangladesh, Nepal, Burma, Assam, Bihar and North Bengal participated in this Conference. The Conference was chaired by Sri Purna Narayan Singh, a former MP from India and the sitting President of Koch-Rajbongshi International Committee. It was resolved that for the overall upliftment of the underprivileged Koch-Rajbongshi, they need to be immediately recognized as Scheduled Tribe in India, and also in the neighbouring states where they inhabit in large number. The Conference also urged upon the cultural integration of the Koch-Rajbongshi with the main stream of the society. The matter of recognition of the Koch-Rajbongshi as ST as such has become an important ethno-political issue in recent years adding new dimension to the social dynamics of the Rajbongshi identity.[36]

Formation of the Rajbongshi Social Identity As A Nationality

Crystallisation of Rajbongshi identity, according to Nandy, became apparent along with hegemonies of Bengali people over the locals. The influx of immigrants from Bangladesh and Bengali Hindus into North Bengal has been on such a large scale that the local population feels overwhelmed. It is alleged that they are depriving the *desi/edesio* (indigenous people alias Rajbongshi) of political as well as socio-economic development. Effectually the Rajbongshi are resisting the domination of Bengalis for their gradual economic marginalization and the erosion of their cultural and linguistic identity. The Rajbongshi do not want to be a part of the population of West Bengal and prefer to have a state of their own called Kamtapur (the name of an early citadel Koch-Rajbongshi). The demand for the recognition of the Kamtapuri language as a separate official language during the last Census (2001) is clear expression of their deliberate move to declare their separate Kamtapuri nationality. Attempts to reconstruct their past history and revive their culture, language and traditions are indications of their nascent nationality consciousness. [37]

Accordingly the Rajbongshi politics of identity for the last one decade has entered into a new phase having two interrelated strands on basic issues but separate in operational spheres. As a political party, Kamtapur Peoples Party in their political proposals has made some radical departures from the various earlier demands of Rajbongshi social identity. It is not caste and religion determining the communitarian politics any longer. It is now culture and language that shape the politics of difference from the dominant Bengali community as a whole in the region. They reject the term Rajbongshi that carries the old Hindu Kshatriya caste association to adopt another term. They have popularized the word 'Kamta' having charged it with historical and cultural connotations. It indicates the area that Kamta and later kings reined for centuries and where the indigenous people spoke the same language and shared the same culture. The language was called Kamtabehari and the culture simply Kamta by Panchanan Barma. This denomination emphasizes the determination of cultural identity, not caste identity, in terms of a region, language and culture. It is on this ground that they claim Rajbongshi have formed a 'nationality'.[38]

However the claim of the Rajbongshi that they constitute a nation or have a separate nationality has been rejected by the West Bengal Government. The argument given by the West Bengal Government is that the Rajbongshi are in fact Bengalis who speak a dialect of the Bengali language. Thus the claim for a separate Rajbongshi identity has been in a way ignored and rejected by the West Bengal Government. Accordingly the stir created by the Rajbongshi for acceptance of their demand for a new Rajbongshi identity has been suppressed by the dominant power elite out of the apprehension that it might ultimately legitimize their claim for a separate territory as a sovereign nation state. The Rajbongshi attribute their deprivation to the hegemonic rule by the power elites mainly belonging to the dominant Bengali community, and consider it completely undemocratic and have expressed resentment against it.[39]

Identity Formation of the Koch Rajbongshi—an Erratic Trajectory

As sociologists Dipankar Gupta pointed out it is the shifting nature of identities that makes cultural boundaries relative in character and rarely absolute. It is particularly during periods of high social tension that identities in moments of peace are usually cast aside for other identities which are shrill, angular, and extremely self-conscious. At such times it is all important to be a Sikh, or a Hindu, or even an Indian, and downsize those other identities of caste, region and sect.[40] To Chandran Kukathas rather than thinking of the world as made up of fixed groups, whose claims need to be considered by those in power, we should begin by recognizing that groups themselves are not permanent or stable entities but more or less temporary associations of individuals. How they associate, who they encompass, and how strong their identities, is determined not simply by their "shared" histories but by the conditions in which they find themselves. Australia's aborigines for instance did not view themselves as a single people before the arrival of European settlers, although now they find themselves united to some degree as a people with a common cause. Differences can be identified along many dimensions from religion to language to ethnicity, although any one of these dimensions might easily supply the basis of a form more or less stable or enduring of social unity.

If identity politics is 'about expressing one's agency and creating new forms of collective agency', then the Rajbongshi did that by playing on the politics of difference and of identity at the same time. Their caste movement was a negotiation of difference to register an altered identity from the projected view about themselves as Koches. But by virtue of that altered identity what it aspired is to be identified with the high-ups in the Hindu caste hierarchy. But another counterforce queered the pitch for them, so much so that it was engulfed in it, proving thereby the presence of a more compelling imperative in them to act as a community/ethnicity rather than a caste. It was enlisting themselves as scheduled caste and joining the Movement. This inevitable contradiction soon eroded the edge and credibility of the Kshatriya movement.[41]The recent move of the Koch-Rajbongshi to demand tribal status is altogether a new phenomenon. It is another manifestation of seeking comfortable accommodation in the institutional framework of protective discrimination. The path of Kshatriyasation for upward social mobility of the Rajbongshi created much tensions and status-anxiety without many benefits in concrete terms. Afterwards their poor economic condition and desire for power and status led to process of downward mobility through aspiration for reservation benefits. The Rajbongshi leaders identified the backward socio-economic status, which is the prime criterion for reservation, contrary to the realization of Kshatriyasation. So Kshatriyasation and reservation appeared to them antithetical to each other. The changing social identity of the Rajbongshi is therefore an obvious manifestation of their erratic position in the caste hierarchy, poor socio- economic condition, and desire for getting suitable accommodation in the institutional framework of protective discrimination.[42] The transition of the Rajbongshi community can be described as a transition from caste to community or ethnicity or even nationality.[43]

To conclude the Rajbongshi in different phases of their identity formation had to bear with disparate Government responses. In the initial phase of their identity formation the response of the Government was promotive; later became accommodative in the colonial era, and has now become somewhat repressive.[44] In social identity construction, such a differential treatment has already created considerable confusion with regard to the Rajbongshi identity.[45] The identity formation of the Koch Rajbongshi can thus be viewed as an erratic trajectory as they demanded Kshatriya status in the regional caste structure but subsequently accepted to be recognised as a Scheduled Caste/OBC that brought them within the purview of preferential treatment at present times.

Notes

1. Rajatsubhra Mukhopadhyay, '*Kshatriyaization Among the Rajbansi: An Appraisal*', Man in India, Volume79 No 3 & 4, July-December, 1999, North Bengal, pp. 347-358.
2. D. Nath, '*The Koches: Their Racial Affinities and Original Homeland*', Journal of Indian History, Volume 64 No.1-3, December, 1986, pp. 175-84.
3. Rajatsubhra Mukhopadhyay, '*Social formation of the Rajbangsi and the Emergence of the* Kamtapuri Identity', in N.K. Das and V.R. Rao ed Identity, Cultural Pluralism and the State: South Asian Perspective, Anthropological Survey of India in association with Macmillan, New Delhi, 2009.
4. Moumita Ghosh Bhattacharyya, 'Rajbangsi: The Deprived People of North Bengal', International Journal of South Asian Studies, Volume 2 No 2, July-December, 2009, Pondicherry University, India.

5. Girindra Narayan Ray, 'The Rajbangsi Identity Politics: The post colonial passages', in ed Social and Political Tensions in North Bengal (Since 1947), N.L. Publishers, Siliguri, West Bengal, 2007.
6. D. Nath, '*The* Koches: Their Racial Affinities and Original Homeland', op.cit.no. 2.
7. Rajatsubhra Mukhopadhyay, '*Social formation of the Rajbangsi and the Emergence of the* Kamtapuri Identity', op.cit.no. 3.
8. Girindra Narayan Ray, 'The Rajbangsi Identity Politics: The post colonial passages', in Sailen Debnath (ed) Social and Political Tensions in North Bengal (Since 1947), N.L. Publishers, Siliguri, West Bengal, 2007.
9. Sailen Debnath, in ed Social and Political Tensions in North Bengal (Since 1947), N.L. Publishers, Siliguri, West Bengal, 2007, pp.44.
10. Rajatsubhra Mukhopadhyay, '*Social formation of the Rajbangsi and the Emergence of the* Kamtapuri Identity', op.cit.no.3.
11. Rajatsubhra Mukhopadhyay, 'Contradiction and Change in Social Identity of the Rajbansis', Journal of Indian Anthropological Society, Volume 34 No.2, July,1999, North eastern Bengal and Assam, pp. 133-138.
12. Moumita Ghosh Bhattacharyya, 'Rajbangsi: The Deprived People of North Bengal', op.cit.no. 4.
13. Rajatsubhra Mukhopadhyay, '*Kshatriyaization Among the Ra*jbansi: An Appraisal', op.cit.no.1.
14. Moumita Ghosh Bhattacharyya, 'Rajbangsi: The Deprived People of North Bengal', op.cit.no.4.
15. Rajatsubhra Mukhopadhyay, '*Social formation of the Rajbangsi and the Emergence of the* Kamtapuri Identity', op.cit.no.3.
16. Rajatsubhra Mukhopadhyay, '*Kshatriyaization Among the Rajbansi: An Appraisal*', op.cit.no.1.
17. Girindra Narayan Ray, 'The Rajbangsi Identity Politics: The post colonial passages', op.cit.no.8.
18. Rajatsubhra Mukhopadhyay, '*Kshatriyaization* among the Rajbansi: an appraisal', op.cit. no.1
19. Girindra Narayan Ray, 'The Rajbangsi Identity Politics: The post colonial passages', op.cit.no. 8.
20. Sailen Debnath, in ed Social and Political Tensions in North Bengal (Since 1947), op.cit.no. 9.
21. Rajatsubhra Mukhopadhyay, '*Kshatriyaization Among the Rajbansi: An Appraisal*', op.cit.no.1.
22. D. Nath, '*The Koches: Their Racial Affinities and Original Homeland*', op.cit.no.2.
23. Rajatsubhra Mukhopadhyay, '*Kshatriyaization* among the Rajbansi: an appraisal', op.cit.no.1.
24. Moumita Ghosh Bhattacharyya, 'Rajbangsi: The Deprived People of North Bengal', op.cit.no.4.
25. Rajatsubhra Mukhopadhyay, '*Kshatriyaization Among the Rajbansi: An Appraisal*', op.cit.no.1.

26. Rajatsubhra Mukhopadhyay, '*Social formation of the Rajbangsi and the* emergence of the Kamtapuri Identity', op.cit.no.3.
27. Rajatsubhra Mukhopadhyay, '*Kshatriyaization Among the Rajbansi: An Appraisal*', op.cit.no.1.
28. Moumita Ghosh Bhattacharyya, 'Rajbangsi: The Deprived People of North Bengal', op.cit.no. 4.
29. The Government of India Act of 1919 constituted the new legal category of social stratum, called 'Depressed Classes', which includes the lower and untouchable castes but also the so-called tribes. In some documents (including the Census of 1931) these groups were also referred 'Exterior Castes'. The Scheduled Castes (SCs) of today were until 1935 called as the Depressed Classes. Op.cit.no. 3.
30. Sailen Debnath, in ed Social and Political Tensions in North Bengal (Since 1947), op.cit.no. 9.
31. Rajatsubhra Mukhopadhyay, '*Social formation of the Rajbangsi and the Emergence of the* Kamtapuri Identity', op.cit.no.3.
32. Sailen Debnath, in ed Social and Political Tensions in North Bengal (Since 1947), op.cit.no.9.
33. Moumita Ghosh Bhattacharyya, 'Rajbangsi: The Deprived People of North Bengal', op.cit.no.4.
34. Sailen Debnath, in ed Social and Political Tensions in North Bengal (Since 1947), op.cit.no.9.
35. Rajatsubhra Mukhopadhyay, '*Social formation of the Rajbangsi and the Emergence of the* Kamtapuri Identity', op.cit.no.3.
36. Sailen Debnath, in ed Social and Political Tensions in North Bengal (Since 1947), op.cit.no. 9.
37. Rajatsubhra Mukhopadhyay, '*Social formation of the Rajbangsi and the Emergence of the* Kamtapuri Identity', op.cit.no. 3.
38. Girindra Narayan Ray, 'The Rajbangsi Identity Politics: The post colonial passages', op.cit.no.8.
39. Rajatsubhra Mukhopadhyay, '*Social formation of the Rajbangsi and the Emergence of the* Kamtapuri Identity', op.cit.no. 3.
40. See Dipankar Gupta, Culture, Space and the Nation-State, Sage Publications, New Delhi, 2000, pp. 102.
41. Girindra Narayan Ray, 'The Rajbangsi Identity Politics: The post colonial passages', op.cit.no. 8.
42. Sailen Debnath, in ed Social and Political Tensions in North Bengal (Since 1947), op.cit.no.9.
43. Girindra Narayan Ray, 'The Rajbangsi Identity Politics: The post colonial passages', op.cit.no. 8.
44. Rajatsubhra Mukhopadhyay, '*Social formation of the Rajbangsi and the Emergence of the* Kamtapuri Identity', op.cit.no.3.
45. Sailen Debnath, in ed Social and Political Tensions in North Bengal (Since 1947), op.cit.no. 9.

Chapter - IV

Kamtapur Movement: Growth and Development

Kamtapur Movement is led by Koch Rajbongshi living in and around Duars and Cooch Behar for a separate state to be carved out of West Bengal namely 'Kamtapur'. Cooch Behar was a princely state prior to its accession to India in 1950. Cooch Behar founded by Viswasingh in 1533 was expanded into the Koch-Kamta Kingdom by King Naranarayan.[1] Under the aegis of the King Naranarayan, a highly centralized administrative structure was prevalent in the Koch-Kamta Kingdom. Goal-oriented development administration was unknown. Later King Harendra Narayan (1783-1840) and Nripendra Narayan (1863-1911) introduced modernism in Cooch Behar with their knowledge of education, literature, music, architecture etc.

Koch-Kamta Kingdom maintained its independent, sovereign status up to 1772. It was turned into a Tributary State under the British India Government in 1773 for its safety from Bhutanese incursions. It however had an autonomous status under the British Rule.[2] King Jagaddipendra Narayan did not support the Congress movement of India against the British and warned his subjects not to revolt against the British Rule. He introduced free education for women for the purpose of the development of women. His measures for education were helpful to raise the consciousness among the people. Cooch Behar Kingdom re-gained independence and sovereign status in his reign for the period from 1947 to 1949 following the Indian Independence Act, 1947.[3]

Hitasadhani Sabha

Cooch Behars's administrative machinery was mainly composed of the educated upper caste Hindu leaders. Although the King was a Rajbongshi yet his administrative machinery did not include the *Deshi* people (Rajbongshi Hindus and Muslims). However Jagaddipendra Narayan for the all round development of Cooch Behar attempted to establish democratic system in Cooch Behar through the local representatives of the people.[4] Accordingly an election was held in the Cooch Behar State. An Organisation named 'Hitasadhani Sabha' was formed on May 19th, 1947 consisting mainly of *Deshi jotedars* (rural landlords) and Rajbongshi elites like Khan Choudhury Amanatulla Ahmed, Satish Chandra Singha Sarkar, and Gajendra Narayan Basunia. With the formation of the Hitasadhani Sabha the aspirations of *Deshi* people received a big fillip. 'Hitasadhani Sabha' contested the election primarily on the issue of the rights of the Rajbongshi against the *Bhatias* (the Rajbongshi Bengalis addressed the immigrant Bengalis from the lower plains of eastern Bengal as *Bhatias*)[5] who because of their education and economic strength were taking upper hands in all socio-economic and administrative matters. The subjects of Cooch Behar were thus divided into *Deshis* and *Bhatias*. *Deshi* people believed that it was because of the *Bhatias* that they were impoverished, and as such there was a call for driving away the *Bhatias* from Cooch Behar. Some upper caste non-*Deshi jotedars* also extended their support to the Hitasadhani Sabha because it served their vested interests. The Movement for awareness and self assertion of the Rajbongshi, as promoted by Panchanan Barma started again under the banner of Hitasadhani Sabha.[6]

'Hitasadhani Sabha' with Khan Choudhury Amanatulla Ahmed as the President contested the election and won all the seats. Khan Choudhury Amanatulla Ahmed and Satish Chandra Singha Sarkar became Council of Ministers along with some non- *Deshi* upper caste Hindu leaders nominated by the King. The *Hita* (Good) or welfare of the Rajbongshi was the motto of the 'Hitasadhani Sabha'. It worked for the Rajbongshi people's right to development. They mainly placed the demands to the Jagaddipendra Narayan, King of Cooch Behar by claiming the right of Rajbongshi in all spheres of development in Cooch Behar. It organised a mass meeting on May 19th, 1946 in the field of Rashmela of Cooch Behar which was attended by the *Deshi* people in large number. In the meeting a proposal was raised to keep Cooch Behar under the Central Government of Indian Dominion for the interest of the development of the local people. It thus initiated the process of transforming Cooch Behar into a centrally administered State.

Post independence the Hitasadhani Sabha adopted the name 'Cooch Behar State Praja Congress'. Hitasadhani Sabha created political enthusiasm among the Rajbongshi by drawing their attention to the fact that the *Deshi* people have been able to capture the power of administration at last and that they can achieve the ultimate goal of administering by themselves in course of time.[7] Reacting to the Government of India's policy of merger of the native state with the nearby big provinces, 'Hitasadhani Sabha' issued a proclamation for an independent Cooch Behar State. On the question of merger of the native state Cooch Behar into the Indian Union the 'Hitasadhani Sabha' opined, "We do not want to mix with any Province either with West Bengal or Assam. Our merger with the so-called province means our extinction; again our separate existence will not remain. We shall miss our Kingdom." Consequently Hitasadhani Sabha launched a movement against the merger of the native state of Cooch Behar with India. Public meetings and processions were organised at Mathabhanga, Mekhliganj, Dinhata, Tufanganj. The 'Hitasadhani Sabha' organised propaganda against the activities of the Congress and other political parties favouring the merger of Cooch Behar with West Bengal.[8]

'Hitasadhani Sabha' thus was the first to demand for a separate homeland of the Rajbongshi community of Cooch Behar. The merger of Cooch Behar as the district of West Bengal resulted in the waning of influence of the 'Hitasadhani Sabha' alias 'Cooch Behar State Praja Congress'. Some of the Muslim members of the 'Hitasadhani Sabha' immigrated to Pakistan. Charges of sedition against India resulted into the expulsion of Amanatullya Khan, Anchhar Uddin Ahmed, Bazle Rahaman, Moqbul Hossain from Cooch Behar. Satish Chandra Roy Singha joined Congress Party and later was elected as an MLA of the West Bengal Assembly as the Minister of the Department of State Transport Corporation. Lack of political consciousness among the Rajbongshi caused no immediate agitation taking the merger of Cooch Behar with West Bengal. The new era of democratic rule started in Cooch Behar along with other parts of India. The people were enthused to experience the people's right in the representative democracy of India.[9]

Uttarakhand Movement

With the incorporation of Cooch Behar in West Bengal the demand of a separate state raised by the Hitasadhani Sabha did not obliterate completely. On October 30th, 1949, the representatives of Cooch Behar State Praja Congress, along with Darjeeling Gorkha League, Sikkim Praja Sammelan and Jalpaiguri Gorkha League organised a meeting at Darjeeling. In the meeting they called for a demand for a separate state named 'Uttarakhand Pardesh Sangha'. Malda and West Dinajpur were not included in the proposed 'Uttarakhand Pradesh Sangha'. 'Uttarkhand' as a nomenclature for a separate state in North Bengal was thus first used in the meeting in Darjeeling in 1949.[10]The demand for the establishment of 'Uttarkhand Pradesh Sangha' was raised before the then Prime Minister Jawaharlal Nehru in 1952 during his visit to Darjeeling. However the demand failed to create a political stir and subsided subsequently.

On July 5th, 1969, Uttarkhand Dal was formed at the Jalpesh temple of Mainaguri of Jalpaiguri District. Panchanan Mallick was the key ideologue to mobilize the Uttarkhand movement. Kalindranath Barman and Sitanath Roy were the front-rank leaders of the Uttarkhand Dal. After the death of Panchanan Mallick, Jugal Kishor organised the activities of the Uttarkhand Dal during its gradual dismemberment. The primary aim of the Uttarkhand Dal was to set apart North Bengal from South Bengal and create a state called 'Kamtapur' within India in order to protect the Rajbongshi from the exploitation of "Calcutta-centric capitalist leaders". They took cue from a large number of examples of union territories which had been created within Indian federal structure depending on language and culture. Among them Maharashtra and Gujarat were eventually developed as separate states in 1960 by partitioning the Bombay Province. In 1962 Nagaland came out as a separate state from Assam. In 1966 Haryana state was formed out of Punjab. Meghalaya was given the status of a separate state in 1971.[11]

The nomenclature 'Uttarkhand' was mainly adopted by the Uttarkhand Dal in view of the fact that a large number of labourers, working in the tea gardens of Jalpaiguri Duars, Malda and West Dinajpur were sympathetic towards the Jharkhand Movement. To acquire the support of the tea garden labourers, the Uttarkhand Dal preferred to take the term '*Khand*' from Jharkhand and thereby named their party 'Uttarkhand'. However for the proposed state for the Rajbongshi the Uttarkhand Dal preferred the nomenclature 'Kamtapur'. In support of the nomenclature 'Kamtapur' they referred to the long historical tradition of North Bengal. In ancient period North Bengal was christened by the name 'Kamtapur'. The five districts of North Bengal—Malda, Dinajpur, Darjeeling, Jalpaiguri and Cooch Behar except the hill regions of Darjeeling comprised the territorial region of the proposed state of 'Kamtapur'. It consisted of a wide area of 8384 square kilometre, which was much greater than many union territories of India from the point of view of area, population and natural resources. Therefore the Uttarkhand Dal viewed their demand of a separate 'Kamtapur' State as legitimate from all respects.[12]

Uttarkhand Dal was the first marked expression of an alternative politics for the Rajbongshi in Cooch Behar. In its inchoate way it moved out of the caste frame and organised itself as a party representing the region in terms of its culture, language and economy that bound the communities together.[13] The Uttarkhand movement was mainly the outcome of the feeling of deprivation of the sons of the soil based on the socio-economic political issues.[14] It emerged out of deliberate and organized efforts on the part of a class of Rajbongshi belonging to the territorial aristocracy and gentry. The Uttarkhand agitation termed the immigrant Bengalis as *Bhatias* and viewed them as their chief competitors in economic, social and political spheres in North Bengal region. Moreover, there existed a belief that even though the Rajbongshi were members of the indigenous community, they were subjected to the domination of an alien population, i.e., the Bengalis. Thus, a kind of intense social distrust against the dominant communities aroused out of a socio- psychological attitude of the Uttarkhand leaders.[15]

The roots of the socio- psychological sense of deprivation among the Uttarkhand leaders can be traced to the colonial settlement policies of land revenue system. It resulted in the transfer of considerable land from the indigenous Rajbongshi *Jotedar* families to the newly emerging elite class of educated immigrants with knowledge of colonial administration. Changes in the land holding led to the withering away of the position of the traditional landed gentry (the Rajbongshi *Jotedars*) who exercised authority as a dominant caste over the rural population in Cooch Behar. The Rajbongshi *Jotedars* viewed the unabated influx of immigrants as the principal cause for the loss of their politico-economic power in Cooch Behar. In the sphere of new economic opportunities, i.e., non-agricultural sector the Rajbongshi *Jotedars* failed to compete with the Bengali immigrants due to lack of education and resources. As a result, a sense of insecurity and discomfort developed among the Rajbongshi *Jotedars* against the migrant communities enjoying a privileged socio-economic and political position in Cooch Behar.

The Uttarkhand movement thus emerged principally out of a common resentment against the already established and politically powerful immigrant population and a common interest of bringing about socio-political development of the Rajbongshi community. The leaders of Uttarkhand movement wanted to channelize their agitation by exploiting the ethnic sentiments of deprivation of the Rajbongshi community.[16] It was more apparent in the case of Uttarkhand movement because its key leaders belonged to the class of territorial aristocracy and gentry in Cooch Behar. Many of them were the members of traditional *Jotedar* families and still depended on landed property for their subsistence. Uttarkhand leaders claimed that *Bargadars* (share-croppers) are totally neglected in the economic sphere of West Bengal. They alleged that the Rajbongshi community is looked down upon by the Bengalis which they should resist. They thus attempted to exploit the Rajbongshi sense of deprivation to the advantage of the Uttarkhand Movement.

Following 'Sahitya Sabha', the principal propagator of the Assam movement, the leaders of Uttarkhand Movement attempted to institutionalise the Movement by appealing to the cultural identity of the Rajbongshi. They appealed to the Rajbongshi to reject the Bengali language as their mother tongue. The inclination towards the revival of Rajbongshi dialect as a distinct language (Kamtapuri) of the region was attempted to establish a distinct identity for the Rajbongshi from the Bengalis of West Bengal. The leaders of Uttarkhand brought the language issue to the fore not only to strengthen the feelings of ethnicity among the Rajbongshi but also to prevent them from being assimilated into the Bengali fold. They alleged the linguistic reorganisation of states resulted into making the Rajbongshi 'minorities' in ethno-linguistic terms in their own territory in spite of having a mother tongue other than the state's language. Accordingly they asserted that at least linguistically there is a sufficient ground to create a separate Kamtapur state.

The Uttarkhand Movement was mainly an outcome of the struggle for power and associated privileges between the indigenous communities (Rajbongshi) and the immigrant Bengalis. Extensive politicisation on class line made considerable dent in the domain of power traditionally enjoyed by the Rajbongshi. Classes rather than castes acted as strong pressure groups in political sphere. In the new political process the leaders moulded in an older milieu lost their age-old supremacy over local power structure. In addition to this, a class of Rajbongshi *Jotedars* were not willing to accept the greater involvement of the immigrant population in the competition for power and authority. They feared that through politicking, the immigrant population will ultimately oust them from the domain of their age-old power and authority in the region. So the claim of a separate Kamtapur state implied that they wanted a favourable condition where the crucial role of other communities (particularly immigrant) in the competitive political process would be minimised and the entire power and authority would come to the grips of the Rajbongshi.

The Uttarkhand Movement thus not only lay in the 'discontent' arising out of 'relative deprivation' but also in the desire to dominate over the immigrant population in socio-economic and political spheres. Changes in the old landholding pattern led to the emergence of a class of new landed elites composed of immigrants to this region. In view of such a situation, when the Rajbongshi were gradually losing their economic power, they attempted to achieve social authority over others by means of Kshatriyaisation. But the failure of the Kshatriyaisation movement to raise their overall social status and authority in the society made the Rajbongshi claim avenues of power and politics. Accordingly to win the struggle for power, the Uttarkhand leaders brought the Kamtapur issue into the forefront. To seek the support of their community they exploited the resentments against the immigrants among the Rajbongshi. The emergence of Uttarkhand Dal and their stir for a separate Kamtapur state thus reflected the desire on the part of a class of Rajbongshi leaders to grab the power and to exert their absolute political authority over everyone.[17] In 1972 the Uttarkhand Dal participated in the Legislative Assembly election in West Bengal. But their candidates were defeated. Their basic issues lost sight in the glare of the dominant progressive ideology of the Left. People got swayed by the Left ideologies, and the Uttarkhand Movement lost ground which was viewed as being guided by the interest of the Rajbongshi *Jotedars* and the elites.[18]

Uttarbanga Tapsili Jati/Upjati Sangathan

In the intermediary period between the decline of the Uttarkhand Dal and the emergence of the Kamtapur Peoples Party, an auxiliary organization named "Uttarbanga Tapsili Jati/Upajati Sangathan" (UTJUS) comprising of Rajbongshi, became the torch-bearer for the redress of their socio-economic and political grievances. Its primary demand was against the citizenship of the Bengali refugees and immigrants from Bangladesh who migrated after 1971. But the organisation lost its influence after the central conference held at Alipurduar Parade Ground in 1986. The conference which was meant to be a peaceful gathering turned volatile with the outbreak of open hostility. The leaders of the conference claimed that the *Bhatia* hoodlums, members of different clubs and the activists of different political parties employed force on participants of the processions injuring hundreds of people, and that the police took no cognizance of the crime. However it was also reported that the leaders of the UTJUS delivered provocative speeches asking the Rajbongshi to reclaim the lands which was occupied by the immigrants from Bangladesh. The outbreak of violence alienated the Rajbongshi from political activities of the UTJUS and discouraged them from holding processions at Alipurduar in the subsequent times. Eventually the existence of UTJUS consigned to oblivion.[19]

Kamtapur Peoples Party

Kamtapur People's Party (KPP) was constituted in 1992. It was an offshoot of the Kamtapur Gana Parishad formed on the lines of the All Assam Students' Union (AASU) and the Asom Gana Parishad (AGP).[20] It was formed with the primary objective of a separate state of Kamtapur for the Rajbongshi within the Indian Union. It was thus a carry-over of the demand and activities by the Uttarkhand Dal in 1970s.

Aims of the Kpp

According to the Constitution of the KPP its aims are as follows:-

1. To revive the vanished tradition, culture, language, literature, folk-ways, folklore of Kamtapur State and to make the Rajbongshi conscious about their own culture and tradition.
2. To drive away the stigma of sub-language or dialect and to revive the status of the 'Kamtapuri' language as a distinct language.
3. To struggle for the development and recognition of Kamtapuri language for the purpose of achieving the organizational goals. The leaders of the KPP formed another sub-organisation known as Kamtapur Bhasa- O- Sahitya Parishad (KBSP) on 1998 in a conference in Kumargram Alipurduar, Jalpaiguri where the KPP raised the following demands-

(a) Inclusion of Kamtapuri language in the 8th Schedule of the Constitution of India.

(b) Improvement of the Kamtapuri literature, by publishing dictionary, grammar books etc. in Kamtapuri language.

(c) Publications of books, novels etc. in Kamtapuri Language.

(d) Correspondence, letters, invitation cards to be written in Kamtapuri Language;

4. The Government of West Bengal failed to develop socio-economic conditions of Kamtapuri people and therefore the task of the KPP is establishment of Kamtapur State for the protection of ethnic identity, culture, language and economic interest of the people.
5. To intensify its drive for collecting new members from among the ethnic Rajbongshi.

Eleven Point Demand of Kpp

The KPP in view of the above mentioned aims has enumerated eleven demands stated below:-

1. In order to enable the Kamtapuri people to govern their own lives by reason of ethnical, lingual, historical and socio-cultural distinction from the rest of the people of West Bengal a separate state namely 'Kamtapur' be created within the framework of Indian Union comprising of whole of North Bengal and adjoining Kamtapuri populated areas of India, in accordance to Article 3 of the Constitution of India.

2. Inclusion of Kamtapuri Language in the Eighth Schedule of the Constitution of India.
3. The Indira- Mujieb Accord for the expulsion of illegal foreigners from Kamtapuri dominated areas of North Bengal be implemented shortly.
4. In order to curb illegal influx of immigrants in North Bengal and adjacent Kamtapuri dominated areas the 'Inner Line Permit' must also be immediately imposed on the areas.
5. With a view to restrain the intrusion of illegal foreigners in North Bengal 'Barbed wire' should be erected on the borderline of both India and Bangladesh without further delay.
6. Cultural programmes of Kamtapuris should be telecast on the television by opening Fulbari Doordarshan sub-Station Centre soon.
7. 'Teesta-Irrigation Project' should be declared as National Project immediately for the all-round development of North Bengal.
8. Cultural programmes of Kamtapuris to be broadcast through 'All India Radio', Siliguri.
9. A Central University namely 'Roy Saheb Thakur Panchanan Barma University' should be set-up in the district of Cooch Behar for the access of higher education by the aboriginal people of North Bengal.
10. Indian enclaves in Bangladesh and Bangladesh enclaves in India are exchanged without further delay.
11. A 'white paper' regarding economic status, culture, population and ethnical identity of the aboriginal people of North Bengal is published immediately with regard to the pre and post history of North Bengal since Independence of India.[21]

Points of Justification For the Demands of Kpp

It is to be noted that the KPP put forward the points of justification of the demands of Uttarkhand for that of Kamtapur which are follows:

1. The major area of North Bengal belongs to Kamtapur, and this area never constituted a part of Bengal; rather, before the advent of the British rule in India, there had been no existence of Bengal as a political entity. Bengal was a province of the Mughal Empire of which Kamtapur was never a part. To stop Bhutanese intrusion and incursion, the kingdom of Koch-Kamtapur signed a treaty

with the British government in 1773. For the reason of not being a part of Bengal, Cooch Behar, Jalpaiguri, and Darjeeling did not become part of British India along with the occupation of Bengal by the British. Kamtapur thus is a political legacy of Rajbongshi, and for the development and prosperity of this zone a new state with the name of Kamtapur is to be established.

2. The Kamtapuri language is neglected. It is not a dialect of Bengali; rather, Kamtapuri language historically preceded the Bengali language which originally was a dialect of *'Rad-Bangla'*. The constitutional recognition of Kamtapuri language is unavoidably necessary. It will be the official language of the proposed Kamtapur state. Kamtapuri language therefore should immediately be incorporated as a medium of instruction at school, college and university level.
3. The natural resources of North Bengal are not used for the progress and prosperity of the inhabitants of this area. The owners of the tea estates are outsiders, and wealth of the forests is reaped by the Government which is South Bengal bound, specifically Calcutta centric. The Government has earned billions of rupees from North Bengal but has made no investment here; money is drained away for investment in a select few southern districts. The Rajbongshi virtually have no share in the huge wealth incurred from their soil. The nature of administration seems to be colonial. As North Bengal is being robbed of her resources, the establishment of a separate state is inevitable for the future of the Rajbongshi.
4. The people of North Bengal, specifically the indigenous Kamtapuris, have no share in the power structure of the state of West Bengal for its cabinet ministers, bureaucrats, capitalists, doctors, engineers, artists and intellectuals are from Calcutta and its adjoining districts, and they consider North Bengal as a sporting ground for exploitation, and the only way of liberation out of it is the struggle for a separate state.
5. North Bengal has become a den of refugees from all directions and this has to be stopped.
6. As to public health and electricity supply, irrigation, education, communication network in North Bengal, nothing has been done for the purpose of meeting the minimal requirement of the people here.[22]

As a political party, KPP was mainly based in the rural areas with the support of the local Rajbongshi in Cooch Behar. It is not caste and religion determining the communitarian politics of the Rajbongshi. It is now culture and language that shape the politics of difference from the dominant Bengali community as a whole in the region. They reject the term Rajbongshi that connotes the old Hindu Kshatriya caste association. They rather prefer the term 'Kamta' having historical and cultural connotations. It indicates the area that Kamta and later kings reined for centuries and where the indigenous people spoke the same language and shared the same culture. The language was called 'Kamtabehari' and the culture 'Kamta'. This denomination emphasizes the determination of cultural identity, not caste identity, in terms of a region, language and culture. It is on this ground that they claim Rajbongshi to have formed a 'nationality', and in terms of the principles of linguistic reorganization of state claim a different state. The name suggested for the state is 'Kamtapur' and the language, 'Kamtapuri'. KPP has stated that the prospective area of Kamtapur is to correspond with the limits of King Jagdipendra Naranarayan's empire; it may thus extend from Kamrup Kamakshya temple to Purnia including Kishanganj of Bihar. It further asserted that the KPP will vehemently resist any plan of the West Bengal Government to include Siliguri sub-division and northern part of the Duars within the jurisdiction of the hill council while conceding to the demand of the GNLF.

The crux of the claim of KPP is contingent upon challenging the dominant discourse that subsumes the Kamtapuri language into Bengali as one of its dialects and the Kamtapuri people to be Bengali by acculturation and assimilation. The Rajbongshi leaders through Kshatriyaisation Movement had aspired to merge into the Varna Hindu hierarchy as Bengali; although that meant abolition of the ethnic identity of the community. The upper caste Bengali Hindu society however did not accept them as Kshatriya 'caste' at all, although the official voice of times called them Bengali for political expediency. This led to vigorous attempt on the part of the KPP leaders as well as the intellectuals of the community to establish their identity in terms of a politics of cultural difference involving attempts to prove that their language, culture, food habit, dress and religious rituals was different from Bengali.[23]

Organisational Structures and Leadership of Kpp

According to the Article VII of the Constitution of the KPP, the organizational structure of the KPP is composed of a Central Committee which is the highest body of the party. It is headed by the party President. Mr. Atul Roy is the present President of the party. The other members of the Central Committee are Lalit Barman, Paresh Roy, Jagodananda Ray,

Nasir Ali Pramanik, and Benimadhab Singh etc. Under the Central Committee there shall be District Committee, Block and Town Committees and *Anchal* or Regional Committee. At the bottom of the party organization, there are village committees. In each of the six districts of North Bengal the District Committees have been formed. The tenure of all these Committees is five years. According to the Article VIII of the Constitution of KPP, 'all the Committees shall have minimum 21 members out of whom sixteen members should be elected and five members would be nominated by the President of the Party'. The KPP also has certain Frontal Organisations such as Kamtapur Youth Association, Kamtapur Labour Organisation, Kamtapur Employees Association, Kamtapur Women's Organisation, etc. Another mentionable Frontal Organisation is Kamtapur Bhash-O-Sahitya Parishad which is in search of the distinctiveness of Kamtapuri Language from other languages viz. the Bengali and Assamese.

Activities of the KPP

The activities of the KPP mainly involve attempts to mobilize people for their demand for a separate state of Kamtapur. Accordingly, several small conferences, meetings and local level demonstrations are held at the grass-root level. Through these meetings and conferences the members of the KPP share their problems, alienation, history of their geographical location, temples etc. making emotional appeals to the masses and creating awareness about the tradition and culture of Kamtapur. A seminar was thus held in Siliguri on language, culture, and socio-economic condition of the North Bengal region in 1998 attended by Mr. Buddhadeb Bhattacharya, former Chief Minister of West Bengal. Several conferences were held in different places of North Bengal such as at Kalin Haat, Dhubguri, Jalpaiguri on May 3rd 1998, Champasari, Siliguri, Darjeeling on December 21st-22nd 1996 and Kumargram, Alipurduar, Jalpaiguri on September 23rd 1977, etc. The intellectuals of the Rajbongshi community came forward to write the history and establish a link between the present and past of the Rajbongshi community. Sanskrit scriptures were widely quoted, legends interpreted, folk songs and ballads rewritten with the objective to build a concrete history of Rajbongshi and raise consciousness about the tradition of Rajbongshi community.[24] The KPP also issues threat to the West Bengal Government of economic blockade declaring that they would prevent transportation of the traditional produce of North Bengal Districts such as tea, oranges, timber, jute-goods, etc., from North Bengal to South Bengal.[25] Besides these the KPP call several strikes or *bandhs* in different places of North Bengal. The KPP also organises several cycle rallies in different parts of North Bengal.

For example, on September 28th 1997 the KPP submitted its eleven point demand charter to the Prime Minister of India, in Delhi and the Divisional Commissioner of North Bengal through a cycle rally.[26]

Split of Kamtapur

In the year 2006 Kamtapur People's Party owing to differences among its leaders split into two factions: Kamtapur People's Party led by Atul Roy and Greater Cooch Behar Movement led by Nikhil Roy. Atul Roy alleged that the Kamtapur Movement and the Greater Cooch Behar Movement are the obverse and the reverse of the same coin; and the split of the Kamtapur People's Party into two factions has not been owing to any ideological and political difference but on account of some unacceptable style of functioning of Nikhil Roy, the leader of the other faction.[27] In spite of the split, the KPP was successful in riveting Government attention to the alienation of the indigenous people from the general projects of development and thereby proved the raison d'être of their agitation in a democratic polity. It was successful to rouse the ethnic emotions of the Rajbongshi community in spite of opposition from the Left progressive Government in West Bengal. It was particularly successful to evolve the discourse of the 'Kamtapuri nationality' on the basis of a common culture, language and region.[28]

Kamtapur Liberation Organisation

Kamtapur statehood movement has not only been guided by the Kamtapur People's Party but also by the Kamtapur Liberation Organisation (KLO), a terrorist outfit, which allegedly came into being with the help of the United Liberation Front of Assam (ULFA).[29] It came into existence on December 28th, 1995. At its inception, the KLO was an over-ground organisation and was formed to address problems such as large-scale unemployment, land alienation, perceived neglect of the Kamtapuri language and identity, and grievances of economic deprivation of the Rajbanshis. But subsequently, its strategy transformed when certain members of the KLO belonging to the All Kamtapur Students' Union (AKSU) organised an armed struggle for a separate Kamtapur State. The objective of the KLO is to carve out a separate Kamtapur State comprising six districts— Cooch Behar, Darjeeling, Jalpaiguri, North and South Dinajpur and Malda—of West Bengal and four contiguous districts of Assam—Kokrajhar, Bongaigaon, Dhubri and Goalpara.[30] However, most of the KLO's activities have been concentrated in Alipurduar in Jalpaiguri and the Siliguri sub-division of Darjeeling. [31] The KLO tries to garner support from the Rajbongshi of Lower Assam (Kokrajhar, Bongaigaon, Dhubri and Goalpara districts), West Garo Hills of Meghalaya and six districts of North Bengal.[32]

Klo-ulfa Nexus

It is alleged by the West Bengal government that there is a close nexus between the KLO and ULFA. The role of ULFA in transforming the character of KLO is considered to be significant. The ULFA, facing an uphill task in terms of maintaining its cadre strength and influence in view of repeated army operations, sought to use the relatively unmanned area of North Bengal for variety of purposes with the help of KLO. First, the area of North Bengal provided ULFA a transit point to commute from Bhutan to Bangladesh and vice versa, while some insurgents crossed over to Nepal through this area. Second, the area was used by ULFA to tranship weapons to their camps in Bhutan. Third, KLO maintained some hideouts for ULFA in this area. Fourth, this area provided a safe haven for injured and battle-weary ULFA cadre. [33] The KLO in turn receives training and support from the ULFA and the National Democratic Front of Bodoland in camps located in the jungles of Southern Bhutan and the Assam-Bengal border.[34]

The Govt of West Bengal suggested as reported by the media that KLO operates in tandem with the ULFA. The KLO taking cue from the ULFA resorted to abductions and extortions of tea planters and businessmen in the North Bengal region. The KLO activists also attacked and killed Communist Party of India-Marxist CPI (M) local leaders and workers.[35] The first KLO-ULFA armed operation as reported by the media was the abduction of a tea garden owner Roshan Lal Garg from Latabari tea estate in Central Duars in July 1999. Garg was released by KLO after the payment of the ransom in February 2000. In November 1999, KLO and ULFA insurgents looted a railway cash counter near Siliguri. In 2000, a joint operation of KLO and ULFA resulted in the deaths of two prominent CPI (M) activists. In June 2000 senior CPI (M) leaders, Sunil Dutta and Dilip Roy were killed at Duramari in Jalpaiguri. In July 2000 CPI (M) supporters, also school teachers, were killed at Mainaguri and Dhupguri. In October 2000 senior lawyer and CPI (M) leader Dipankar Ghosh was killed. In 2001 CPI (M) leader Sudhir Burman and three Revolutionary Socialist Party (RSP) leaders were gunned down. On August 7th 2000, a CPM activist Nitai Das was killed at Jalpaiguri. In October 2000, a tea garden owner Om Prakash Agarwal was abducted by a joint team of KLO and ULFA insurgents. KLO, along with ULFA, called for a boycott of the Republic Day celebrations on January 26th, 2001 from 1 a.m. till 6p.m. with the proclaimed objective of overthrowing the Indian colonial rule.[36] The KLO in collaboration with the ULFA encamped in the jungles of southern Bhutan and began to use the forest paths of North Bengal as invisible corridors before and after every operation. From Teesta to Kumargram, the entire

Duars became unsafe for the Leftists mainly for the CPI (M) activists and supporters. The police did not have noticeable success against the terrorists for they had no training in counter-insurgency tactics and in the use of automatic weaponry frequently used by the terrorists.[37]

Operation Flush Out

KLO suffered a major setback with the 'Operation Flush Out' of Royal Bhutanese Army (RBA). RBA destroyed its camps in the India-Bhutan border and captured five of its most senior leaders. The RBA handed over to the Indian authority the founder-members of KLO Joydeb Roy alias Tom Adhikari and Milton Burman alias Mihir Das, and other important leaders such as Sanjoy Adhikari alias Vicky, Bhim Dakua alias Jayanta Das and Pabitra Singha alias Biplab Singha. While Tom Adhikari was the action squad head of the organisation, Milton Burman, the second-in-command after Tamir Das alias Jiban Singha was the tactician. Tom Adhikari masterminded the attack on the local office of the Communist Party of India (Marxist) in Dhupguri town in Jalpaiguri district on August 17th, 2003, in which five CPI (M) workers were killed and 14 others injured. Also involved in the attack were Jiban Singha and ULFA activist Biju Chakraborti. Tom Adhikari and Chakraborti were also responsible for the murder of Democratic Youth Federation of India (DYFI) leader Charan Thakur on October 11th, 2003, in Banchukamari Haat, Jalpaiguri. 'Operation Flush Out' put out of action seven of the 10 members of the KLO core committee.[38]

Interrogation of the five captured leaders of KLO uncovered new information about the banned outfit's activities. Contrary to the widely held notion that the KLO was financed by Pakistan's Inter-Services Intelligence (ISI), interrogations revealed that the outfit's arms and ammunition were purchased from Bangladeshi arms dealers and supplied by ULFA. Although the ULFA trained KLO militants, it hardly ever involved itself directly in the latter's 'operations'. The KLO, in turn, would pay for the training and the arms and help arrange rations and other supplies to ULFA. Interrogations further confirmed KPP's link with KLO. The captured militants confessed financing the KPP. However it was revealed that the two organisations, although close to each other, had different political agendas. While the KPP demanded only a separate State of Kamtapur, the KLO wanted a separate country carved out of parts of North Bengal and Assam.[39]

However the recourse to violence has alienated a large number of Rajbongshi intellectuals from the Movement of KLO. The KPP too distanced itself from the KLO since January 2001 when KLO along with all militant groups operating from the region gave a call to boycott the Republic Day celebrations.[40] The support base of KLO also suffered a setback due to the presence of other Kamtapuri political organisations such as the KPP, All Kamtapur Students Union (KSU), the Kamtapur Women's Right Front (KWRF) in West Bengal fighting for the cause of Rajbongshi.[41]The KLO now operates independently of the KPP.

Greater Cooch Behar Peoples Association

The movement for the separate state of Rajbongshi is also being spearheaded by the 'Greater Cooch Behar People's Association' (GCPA) formed on September 9th 1998 at Kakbari school under the leadership of Bangshi Badan Barman. GCPA, however, gained momentum in the second half of 2005 as the KPP weakened due to a split in the party. The GCPA claimed to be a development-oriented organisation and started mobilising the Rajbongshi ethnic community and other ethnic minorities in the region on the issue of a separate state of Greater Cooch Behar. Like KPP it is also demanding a separate state called 'Greater Cooch Behar' with the areas of present Cooch Behar and parts of Dinajpur, Jalpaiguri, Darjeeling and Assam. The language of this new state according to GCPA will be Kamtapuri or the Cooch Behari language. They are doing so in reference to the history, cultures and tradition of ancient Cooch Behar.[42] They derived its legacy from the 'Hita Sadhani Sabha'; and the former Cooch Behar state in its pristine form is its *espirit de corps.*

The GCPA argument is that King Jagaddipendra Narayan signed the document for merger of Cooch Behar with India only and not specifically with West Bengal. They claim that after the King signed the instrument of accession, Cooch Behar enjoyed the status of a province; therefore, the option of returning Cooch Behar to the status of a province or union territory by revoking its merger with West Bengal still remains, and that Cooch Behar be declared a separate state.[43] GCPA pointed out that Cooch Behar was regarded as a C-category state during the period of merger with India. Accordingly as per the Indian Constitution, Cooch Behar was to be centrally administered. But the Central Government did not do so. Rather it was unconstitutionally turned into a district of West Bengal. So the GCPA demands the status quo of the state of Cooch Behar as a separate state.[44]

Demands of The Greater Cooch Behar Movement

The demands of the GCPA as per the Memorandum submitted to Union Home Minister on June 18th, 2005 and their leaflet "*Danga Kuchbihar Basir*

Koyta Katha" (A few submissions of Greater Cooch Behar people) are as follows:-

1. The Maharaja of Cooch Behar had not, of his own, agreed to the accession of the State to the Dominion of India.
2. In terms of the Instrument of Accession signed on August 28th, 1949 and August 30th, 1949 Cooch Behar State can never be merged with West Bengal. Vide D.O.No. 15 (19)-P/49 DT.30.8.49 V.P. Menon, the Indian Government representative communicated its intention to administer the State centrally by a Chief Commissioner.
3. In terms of Section 7 (1) of the Indian Independence Act, 1947, the British Government abolished all the agreements entered into during the period 1773 to 1902 by which the British Empire occupied the areas of present Darjeeling, Jalpaiguri, Uttar and Dakshin Dinajpur and Goalpara district of Assam which constituted the territories of Greater Cooch Behar.
4. In terms of the Instrument of Accession, Cooch Behar has been a C-category State which cannot be merged with West Bengal, an A-category State by a notification under section 290A of the Government of India Act, 1935.
5. In the agreement, the Government of India has communicated that it can take no important decision without Cooch Behar People's mandate. In terms of the agreement, Government of India is promise-bound to meet the problems of Cooch Behar people.

In the perspective of the above submissions, the GCPA demanded implementation of the conditions of Instrument of Accession by virtue of which Cooch Behar State has remained a C-category State. According to GCPA, the agreement contains the history, tradition, language and culture of the people of Cooch Behar and the commitments about the communal harmony and rights to food, shelter, health and education of the people. As such their slogan is –"*Kuchbiharer Bharat Bhukti Chukti Kuchbihar basir Mukti*" (Instrument of Accession is the salvation of Cooch Behar people). Hence their immediate demand is not to force upon the people of Cooch Behar the unconstitutional election of West Bengal Assembly and implement the Instrument of Accession at the earliest.[45]

Activities of Greater Cooch Behar Peoples Association

The GCPA in order to reiterate their demand for a separate state have involved in submission of memorandum, picketing and demonstration. They have submitted memorandums to political leaders like A B Vajpayee, former Prime Minister of India and Sonia Gandhi, President of All India Congress Committee. It was during West Bengal Legislative Assembly elections, 2006 that GCPA demanded the formation of an interim caretaker government in Cooch Behar by the Union Government. However in view of no response from the government of West Bengal, the GCPA boycotted the West Bengal Assembly elections in 2006 asserting that the political status of the Cooch Behar is still not clear. In its memorandum to Sonia Gandhi dated August 27th, 2008 GCPA expressed that the people of Cooch Behar have lost their prosperity and future in their own land.

They have also adopted the method of non- cooperation to assert their demand. Accordingly farmers in Cooch Behar refused to pay the land taxes to the West Bengal government on the insistence of GCPA in July, 2005. They organised demonstration in Jantar Mantar, New Delhi on December 11th and 12th, 2014 to draw attention to their demand to restore the earlier status of Category 'C' statehood or grant Union Territory status to Greater Cooch Behar.[46] The GCPA although did not articulate the economic content of their demands but was successful in mobilising the poor rural population of the Cooch Behar consisting mainly of Rajbongshi ethnic community. It has also been successful in enlisting the support of Atul Roy's Kamtapur People's Party (KPP) who quoted in The Statesman dated April 22nd, 2007 that KPP was not averse to the proposed state being named as Cooch Behar.[47]

Greater Cooch Behar Democratic Party

The GCPA formed a political party named 'The Greater Cooch Behar Democratic Party' (GCDP) on June 24th, 2006 at Dinhata Nripendra Narayan Smriti Sadan.[48] According to the members of the GCDP, the mother organization i.e. The Greater Cooch Behar Peoples Association was not involved in the electoral process. But later, members of the GCPA felt that participation in the democratic electoral process is necessary to press for their demand for a separate state. Thus, the Greater Cooch Behar Democratic Party was formed out of its mother organization the Greater Cooch Behar Peoples Association. But for all practical purpose both these organization, actually represent the same group of people and their demands.[49] Accordingly a memorandum to declare the Cooch Behar as a state under the Union of India was put forward by GCDP to the President of India dated January 7th, 2009.[50] The GCDP contested the Lok Sabha elections of 2009; its candidate, Bangshi Badan Barman, contested as an independent candidate and secured 37,226 votes.[51]

Greater Kamta United Forum

Atul Roy the leader of the Kamtapur Progressive Party set up an organizational connection with the GCDP and both the parties in alliance have formed the 'Greater Kamta United Forum' in order to exert greater pressure on the Government for their common demand of a separate state for the Rajbongshi. Atul Roy considers the Greater Cooch Behar Movement as an alternative mobilization force with the reflection of most of the demands of the KPP. Thus the demands of the GCPA, GCDP and that of the KPP, in course of time, may coalesce together to the effect of organising a more organized Kamtapur Movement.[52]

To conclude, the demand of separate state for the Rajbongshi started by the Hitasadhani Sabha is gathering momentum day by day. The Hitasadhani Sabha was limited only to the Hindu and Muslim *Jotedars* of the period and the area of its proposed state were concentrated to Cooch Behar only. But in later years the movement acquired a strong mass support and expanded to different areas of North Bengal demanding a separate state comprising the five districts of North Bengal. The movement also changed its name from time to time in tune with circumstances. Language issue was not raised by the Uttarkhand movement. But the language issue has been the single biggest factor behind the growth of the KPP and the subsequent movements for a separate state of Kamtapur. They demanded introduction of Kamtapuri language as well as inclusion of their history in the history syllabus of the North Bengal University. However the prime goal of the Hitasadhani Sabha, the Uttarkhand Party, Kamtapur Gana Parishad, Kamtapur People's Party and Greater Cooch Behar Movement was the same—to set up a separate state of Kamtapur.[53]

Notes

1. Parbananda Das, '*The Hitasadhanee Sabha and the Tensions of Cooch Behar's integration with India*', in Sailen Debnath edited Social and Political Tensions in North Bengal (Since 1947), N.L. Publishers, Siliguri, West Bengal, 2007.
2. Dilip Kumar Sarkar, *'Integrated Decentralization: A Case of Cooch Behar District in West Bengal'*, Journal of Indian Anthropology, Volume XXV No.2 and Volume XXVI No.1 January-December, 1998.
3. Parbananda Das, '*The Hitasadhanee Sabha and the Tensions of Cooch Behar's integration with India*', op.cit.no.1.
4. Parbananda Das, '*The Hitasadhanee Sabha and the Tensions of Cooch Behar's integration with India*', op.cit.no.1.
5. Rajatsubhra Mukhopadhyay, *'Uttarkhand Movement: A Sociological Analysis'*, Special Lecture VIII, Centre for Himalayan Studies, University of North Bengal, West Bengal, 27 February, 1987.

6. Anirban Biswas, '*Destination Kamtapur*', Frontier, Volume 35 No 20, 2002, pp.9-10.
7. Ibid.
8. Parbananda Das, '*The Hitasadhanee Sabha and the Tensions of Cooch Behar's integration with India*',op.cit.no.1.
9. Ibid.
10. Rajatsubhra Mukhopadhyay, '*Uttarkhand Movement: A Sociological Analysis*', op.cit.no. 5.
11. Ibid.
12. Rajatsubhra Mukhopadhyay, '*Uttarkhand Movement: A Sociological Analysis*', op.cit.no.5.
13. Girindra Narayan Ray, '*The Rajbanshi Identity Politics: The Post Colonia Passages*', in Sailen Debnath, ed Social and Political Tensions in North Bengal (Since 1947), N.L. Publishers, Siliguri, West Bengal, 2007.
14. Sukhbilas Barma, '*Social and Political Tension in North Bengal since—1947*', in Sailen Debnath, in ed Social and Political Tensions in North Bengal (Since 1947), N.L. Publishers, Siliguri, West Bengal, 2007.
15. Rajatsubhra Mukhopadhyay, '*Uttarkhand Movement: A Sociological Analysis*', op.cit.no. 5.
16. Ibid.
17. Ibid
18. See Sukhbilas Barma, '*Social and Political Tension in North Bengal since—1947*', op.cit.no.14.
19. Sailen Debnath, ed Social and Political Tensions in North Bengal (Since 1947), N.L. Publishers, Siliguri, West Bengal, 2007, pp. 49-50.
20. Rajatsubhra Mukhopadhyay, '*Uttarkhand Movement: A Sociological Analysis*', op.cit.no.5.
21. Kamal Chandra Barman, '*Ethnic Movements in North Bengal: A Review of Kamtapur and Greater Cooch Behar State Demand in Cooch Behar*', unpublished MPhil dissertation, University of North Bengal, 2007.
22. See Sailen Debnath, ed Social and Political Tensions in North Bengal (Since 1947),op.cit.no.19, pp. 50-52.
23. Girindra Narayan Ray, '*The Rajbanshi Identity Politics: The Post Colonia Passages*', op.cit.no.13.
24. See Sailen Debnath, ed Social and Political Tensions in North Bengal (Since 1947),op.cit.no.19.
25. Jaydeep Mitra, 'Lack of Development gives rise to Separatist Sentiments', http: //www.cpiml.org /liberation/year_2001/February/ 06%20special%20 report. Html.
26. See Sailen Debnath, ed Social and Political Tensions in North Bengal (Since 1947), op.cit. no. 19.
27. See Sailen Debnath, ed Social and Political Tensions in North Bengal (Since 1947), op.cit.no.19, pp. 55-56.

28. Girindra Narayan Ray, *'The Rajbanshi Identity Politics: The Post Colonia Passages'*, op.cit.no.13.
29. Anirban Biswas, '*Destination Kamtapur'*, op.cit.no. 6.
30. Barun Roy, *'Datasheet: Kamtapur Liberation Organisation'*, November 12, 2008, http: //beacononline. wordpress.com /2008/11/12/ datasheet-Kamtapur-liberation-organisation-klo/.
31. Suhrid Sankar Chattopadhyay, *'A Ruthless Hit Squad'*, Frontline, Volume 21 No 1, January 03-16, 2004.
32. Bibhu Prasad Routray, '*Kamtapur Liberation Organisation'*, http: //indianarmy. nic.in/Site/Form Templete/ frmTemp SimpleWithFourPara.aspx? MnId = X5osxuOq lY0= & Parent ID= KDe + m3 KVGiw.
33. Ibid.
34. Suhrid Sankar Chattopadhyay, *'A Ruthless Hit Squad'*, op.cit.no.31.
35. Bibhu Prasad Routray, '*Kamtapur Liberation Organisation'*, op.cit.no.32.
36. Ibid.
37. Anirban Biswas, '*Destination Kamtapur'*, op.cit.no.6.
38. Suhrid Sankar Chattopadhyay, *'A Ruthless Hit Squad'*, op.cit.no.31.
39. Bibhu Prasad Routray, '*Kamtapur Liberation Organisation'*, op.cit.no.32.
40. Alok Kumar Gupta & Chanda Saswati, '*Kamtapur Liberation Organization'*, Third Concept, *Volume* 16 No 191, January, 2003.
41. Bibhu Prasad Routray, '*Kamtapur Liberation Organisation'*, op.cit.no.32.
42. See Arun K. Jana, *'Backwardness and Political Articulation of Backwardness in the North Bengal Region of West Bengal'*, in Ashutosh Kumar's edited Rethinking State Politics in India: Regions within Regions, Routledge, New Delhi, 2011.
43. Anirban Biswas, '*Destination Kamtapur'*, op.cit.no.6.
44. Ibid
45. See Sukhbilas Barma, *'Social and Political Tension in North Bengal since—1947'*, op.cit.no.14.
46. See Annexure No. III.
47. See Arun K. Jana, *'Backwardness and Political Articulation of Backwardness in the North Bengal Region of West Bengal'*, op.cit.no. 42.
48. Anirban Biswas, '*Destination Kamtapur'*, op.cit.no. 6.
49. See Sailen Debnath, ed Social and Political Tensions in North Bengal (Since 1947), op.cit.no.19.
50. See Annexure No. II
51. Op.cit.no.46
52. See Arun K. Jana, *'Backwardness and Political Articulation of Backwardness in the North Bengal Region of West Bengal'*, op.cit.no.42.
53. Rajatsubhra Mukhopadhyay, *'Uttarkhand Movement: A Sociological Analysis'*, op.cit.no.5.

Chapter - V

Kamtapur Movement and Cultural Diversity in West Bengal: Challenges Ahead

Kamtapur movement is an autonomy movement for the separate state of Kamtapur by the Rajbongshi in North Bengal. Kamtapur is an imaginary state for the Koch Rajbongshi with no material existence. This imagination is largely based on their belief on the existence of such a state in the ancient history dating back to the 13th century. Accordingly the Koch Rajbongshi do not name their proposed state on the name of their community, rather they derive the imagination or the idea of Kamtapur from history. According to their history, Kamtapur was the capital of the Karumpa kingdom which constituted of the present day Assam together with West Bengal. The Rajbongshi of North Bengal tends to identify themselves to this Kamtapur Kingdom which is a historical reality and not the present West Bengal state of which they now form a part of. Accordingly various organisations like KPP, KLO and Greater Cooch Behar Party have been demanding a separate state for the Koch Rajbongshi to preserve and maintain their distinct identity and a glorious past.[1]

Princely State of Cooch Behar: A Brief History

Cooch Behar or "land of the Koches" once formed part of the ancient kingdom of Kamrupa. The Kamta kingdom appeared in the western part of the older Kamarupa kingdom in the 13th century, after the fall of the Pala dynasty. The rise of the Kamta kingdom marked the end of the ancient period in the history of Assam and the beginning of the medieval period. The first rulers were the Khens, who were later displaced by Alauddin Hussain Shah, the Turko-Afghan ruler of Bengal. Though Hussain Shah developed extensive administrative structures, he could not maintain political control which eventually went to the Koch dynasty. The Koch Rajbongshi's called themselves Kamateshwars (the rulers of Kamta/Kamtapur Kingdom), but their influence and expansions were so extensive and far reaching that their kingdom is sometimes called the Koch kingdom.[2] It was so called after the Koches had established their political predominance under Biswa Singha in the earlier half of the 16th century. It was under Nara Narayan (1534-87) that Cooch Behar reached the apex of its glory.

The struggle between the Koch and the Bhutanese is recorded by the British anthropologist Dalton who stated, "There were no doubt conflicts between the Kutch and the Bhutias about three hundred or four hundred years ago but these were struggles for supremacy in the Duars which ended in many of the Kutch leaders as Sidli and Bijni and other chiefs submitting to the Bhutias."Bhutan's interest in the affairs of Cooch Behar throughout the 18th century centred on ensuring her hold over the fertile tract now known as the Western Duars. Historically, these Duars extending from river Teesta to Sankos and beyond were held by Koch chieftains. The late H N Chaudhuri, in his official history of Cooch Behar reported that the Bhutanese systematically took possession of a large of number of "*taluks*" (a land unit) in the Western Duars. He remarked that these areas "formerly held in farm under Cooch Behar, were usurped by them and the payment of revenue was stopped. They also openly dispossessed some other lands covered by *taluks* Chichakhata, Paglahat, Luckiduar, Kyranti and Maraghat which were under direct management of the state". This remark throws a flood of light on the process through which the Bhutanese acquired control over the Duars under Cooch Behar though it lacks the basis of firm chronology.

The Koch monarchy had lost its vitality as a result of division and internecine strife during the early 16th century. Chiefs like the Raikats of Baikunthopur were virtually independent and made a bid to settle old scores by capturing the metropolis, Cooch Behar. It was in this period of instability that the hill kingdom of Bhutan embarked on its systematic expansion in the plains of the Duars adjoining the hills. Territorial expansion convinced the Bhutanese that permanent hold over the Duars could not be retained without extending their political hegemony over Cooch Behar. There were extensive tracts in Maraghat and Chamurchi in the possession of Cooch Behar. By the middle of the 18th century Bhutanese presence in Cooch Behar was so extensive that and they even influence the process of formation of monarchy. It was with Bhutanese assistance that Maharaja Upendra Narayan (1714-63) defeated the Mughal army that attacked Cooch Behar in support of Dinnarayan. In 1765 the royal preceptor Ramananda, who had conspired in the assassination of Maharaja Devendra Narayan was taken prisoner and later executed by the Bhutanese in Punakha. Thereafter a Bhutanese representative, Pensu Toma, was stationed in Cooch Behar and he began to interfere directly in the affairs of its administration.

In 1770 the Bhutanese King Desi Shidariva descended on the plains of Buxa and took prisoner Maharaja Dhairjendra Narayan. An appeal from Nazir Khagendra Narayan on behalf of minor Dharendra Narayan evoked prompt response from the British governor general Warren Hastings in colonial India. The Bhutanese were dangerously near the British district of Rangpur, and Cooch Behar as a buffer could be lost forever. Moreover the prospects of commercial relations with Tibet through Bhutan had kindled Hastings' imagination. Incidentally, the war with Bhutan was the "first move in the diplomatic game" to secure commercial access in Tibet. The aim of the British in the first Anglo Bhutanese war therefore was nothing less than extending their possession to the "foot of the hills on the side". A British army of four companies under Captain Jones arrived and the First Bhutan War began. The capture of Cooch Behar in 1772 was a decisive event in the war. The ensuing Anglo Cooch Behar Treaty of 1772 ensured British paramount over Cooch Behar wherein the Bhutanese aim of political predominance in Cooch Behar had been successfully checked. Once British control over Cooch Behar was ensured by the Anglo Cooch Behar Treaty of 1772 the interests of Trans-Himalayan trade widened the gulf between Cooch Behar and Bhutan. Since 1773 the princely state of Cooch Behar was not allowed either to negotiate independently or to take action on its own to prevent lawlessness on the border. The jurisdiction of the courts of Cooch Behar to try criminals in the Duars was denied. As the paramount power in Cooch Behar the British Government was under an obligation to protect the subjects of the Raja in the Duars.[3]

Cooch Behar's Merger with Independent India

With India's independence in 1947, Sardar Patel, Home Minister of the newly independent India on the basis of the 'Instrument of Accession' secured the merger of most of the Indian princely states with India. With regard to the accession of the princely state of Cooch Behar there surfaced intricate problems as to its modalities. The idea of its merger either with India or with Pakistan received diverse reactions. The Bengali Hindu immigrants in Cooch Behar with the modernization of the Cooch Behar state under the leadership of Nripendra Narayan had entrenched themselves in power. They expressed interest with the merger of Cooch Behar with India. While the Muslims, who constituted about forty percent of the population, favoured the option of Cooch Behar's merger with Pakistan.

The Rajbongshi who had traditional exclusiveness with the immigrant Hindus succinctly expressed their desire to constitute Cooch Behar either as a Union Territory with some special rights or its merger with Assam but not West Bengal. The Muslim leaders in order to secure the support of the Rajbongshi emphasised on linguistic and cultural affinities between the Hindus and Muslims of Cooch Behar. While the immigrant Hindus with the objective of ascertaining the inclusion of Cooch Behar as a district of West Bengal manipulated Bidhan Chandra Roy, Chief Minister of West Bengal to influence Sardar Patel in favour of merger of Cooch Behar with West Bengal. Deliberate measures were thus adopted by the immigrant Hindus to vitiate the other two moves in favour of Pakistan and Assam respectively. Thus with regard to the status of Cooch Behar there appeared four options:-

1. Merger with India as a district of West Bengal.
2. Merger with India as the district of Assam.
3. Merger with India as Union Territory.
4. Merger with Pakistan.[4]

Following the partition of India the power to decide the status of the princely states rests with the Government of Independent India. Pt Jawaharlal Nehru, the Prime Minister of the newly independent India, favoured merger of the native states with the neighbouring big provinces of India. As a result, the unrest among the native states accrued. Cooch Behar King too was thoughtful of its prospective political status. Muhammad Ali Jinnah, first Governor General of Pakistan expressed the interest of Pakistan to come to treaty—relations with the native states comprising of favourable terms and treatment as independent states. Jinnah assured the native states of their full separate existence in Pakistan.

In 1946 the Kings of the native states formed a 'Confederation of Native States' as a parallel state to India. Some of the native states got inclined to Pakistan in the context of Jinnah's assurance of independent status in Pakistan. However given the fact that most of the Kings of the native states belonged to Hindu community the Confederation gave liberty to the native states to decide their merger with India and Pakistan respectively. The Indian Government wanted to determine the fate of Cooch Behar by plebiscite. Gopinath Bardoloi, the Chief Minister of Assam and Nilmani Phukan, Assamese laureate suggested the Government to merge Cooch Behar with Assam. The Congress Committee of Assam demanded the merger of Cooch Behar with Assam emphasizing the affinity in the language and culture of both the regions. Meanwhile Sarat Chandra Bose of West Bengal established the 'Socialist Republican Party' and tried to merge Cooch Behar with West Bengal. Kailash Nath Katju, the then Governor of West Bengal in his report to Sardar Patel alleged, 'there have been all sorts of reports in the newspapers about the developments in Cooch Behar. It was suggested that the Muslims from Pakistan were infiltrating into Cooch Behar and some reports went to the length of suggesting that there would be a definite attempt to make Cooch Behar join Pakistan and this movement would be repugnant to the Ruling House.' He advised Sardar Patel to merge Cooch Behar with West Bengal, so that the election-process would be favourable to Congress competing against Socialist Republican Party of Sarat Chandra Bose in West Bengal Assembly elections. Mass signature campaign in West Bengal was organised in favour of the merger of Cooch Behar with West Bengal. The signatories were—Aruna Dasgupta, Sasadhar Kar, Bipul Chandra Bandyopadhyay, Satish Chandra Bhowmik, Khagendra Nath Dasgupta, Abani Saha Neogi, Narendra Nath Mahalanabish etc. Thus both the states of Assam and West Bengal made deliberate attempts to merge Cooch Behar to their respective states. King Jagaddipendra Narayan however tried to maintain Cooch Behar's separate existence in spite of the fact that the native states of small nature merged with the neighbouring big provinces in India, as Jaipur, Udaipur, Bharatpur, Jodhpur were included in Rajastan, Punjab was formed of Patiala and merging native states of East Punjab and native states of Shimla, etc.

Amidst this, on June 12th, 1949, the Congress Committee of Assam decided to merge Cooch Behar with Assam emphasizing the affinity in language and culture. But the State Congress of Cooch Behar decided that there is connection of Cooch Behar with Bengali language and culture and that Cooch Behar must be merged with West Bengal. K. N. Katju, Governor of West Bengal informed Rajagopalachari, Governor General of Indian Dominion to take step immediately for the merger of Cooch Behar with West Bengal in apprehension of the pressures by the supporters of Assam Congress Committee for the merger of the native state of Cooch Behar with Assam. On July 14th, 1949 Pt. Nehru declared in Calcutta, "The question of the merger of Cooch Behar would be decided according to the wish of the people." The West Bengal State Congress and Prajamandal Dal created pressure for the merger of Cooch Behar with West Bengal in consideration of affinity with Bengali language and culture. K. N. Katju, Governor of West Bengal informed Sardar Patel that the attempt was being made to join Cooch Behar with Pakistan by causing infiltration of the Muslims.[5] In such disconcerted situation, King Jagaddipendra Narayan of Cooch Behar became anxious to achieve the better of the four options. His profound relations with the intelligentsia of Calcutta and the gradual pressures from within and outside ultimately resulted into the signing of Instrument of Accession by King Jagaddipendra Narayan on September 28th, 1949 on condition of some privileges to Cooch Behar by the Government of India. Cooch Behar became a district of West Bengal. Things passed easier with no reports of communal violence, and after the merger King Jagaddipendra Narayan lived more than two decades only to breathe his last in 1970.[6]

Cooch Behar in Early Independence Era

Independence of India although triumphant was shrouded in uncertainty as no major strands of the national movement had a clearly worked out plan with regard to how the state would run after British colonialism was ended. Different points of view were put forward from time to time such as the establishment of Planning Commission later known as the Mahalanobis model of statist intervention to modernize the economy. The Congress party leaders appeared indefinite particularly with the territorial issues in pre-Independence days allowing for national self-determination and the parcelization of territory. Jawaharlal Nehru said in a letter to Sir Stafford Cripps: 'Finally if a definite area expresses its will clearly in favour of separatism and this is feasible, no compulsion will be exercised to force it to remain in the Federation or Union'. The nationalist leaders were unsure not only of the territorial issues but also of the question whether the structure of the state would be a 'Federation or a Union'.

Independence followed by Partition witnessed that the sense of common participation had faded into oblivion. Partition had heightened the consciousness of territory. It led to the popular consciousness about the territorial lineaments among the masses who grieved the brutalities and destruction that took place on both sides of the border. Given the Partition and its immediate aftermath secessionist activity was thereby considered criminal. Subsequently the easy accession of Princely India to British India demonstrated the popular endorsement over territory. This searing of consecrated territory into India's national consciousness was challenged by the affirmation of cultural space from all quarters of India—including Kashmir. However after the Partition no allowances were made for democratic assertions of any kind towards national self-liberation. If in the past such ideas of self determination were not resisted, it now became a criminal offence to espouse them. The Indian government rather systematically and relentlessly integrated the erstwhile princely provinces into the Indian union.

Territory signifies cultural space within which the community aspires towards common goals. Accordingly the alienation of territory is difficult for nation-states to bear. Since the concept of territory is based on shared participation, a common grief, and a common mission, it is most likely that a nation-state cobbled together primarily on the basis of historic agreements is fragile in character. Historic agreements fail to replace strong centripetal sentiments which gird and underpin the nation-state. In the Indian case, for example, Kashmir's accession to India was the result of a historic agreement. The inclusion of North-East regions into India was also not an outcome of sentiment welling up in those areas, but rather had military and strategic reasons. Accordingly these regions have been the hotbed for many volatile secessionist as well as separatist movements. Internationally Canada provides a classic case where the problem of making a nation-state on the basis of historic agreements shows up very clearly in the tensions between French Quebec and English Canada. Thus wherever historic agreements have been arrived at, special care has to be taken to involve those regions in the larger membership of the nation-state.[7]

The inclusion of the princely state of Cooch Behar earlier known as Kamta Kingdom into the Indian state was also based on historic agreement between Maharaja Jagaddipendra Narayan of Cooch Behar and the Government of Independent India. It is found that from 1765 to 1783, the interference of the Bhutanese in the affairs of Kamta Kingdom and their frequent attacks on the Kingdom had become prominent. To get rid of the Bhutanese intrusion King Dharmendra Narayan signed a defense treaty with East India Company on April 5, 1773. As a consequence of this treaty, Cooch Behar became a native state of the British India and continued to remain so till 1947. Cooch Behar as an Indian State was ruled by the Maharaja of Cooch Behar who had been a feudatory prince under the British Government. By a document dated August 28th, 1949 Maharaja Jagaddipendra Narayan of Cooch Behar ceded his territory to the Dominion of the Government of India. With the transfer of the administration to the Government of India on 12th day of September 1949 Cooch Behar was ruled as a Chief Commissioner's Province by a Chief Commissioner appointed by the Government of India. By an order under section 290A of Government of India Act of 1935, Cooch Behar was transferred and merged with the Province of West Bengal on January 1st, 1950. Since then Cooch Behar is being administered as a district of West Bengal.[8]

Lefebvre talks about 'imagined space'. Imaged spaces 'are mental invention and comprises codes, signs, utopian places, landscapes, as well as material constructs such as symbolic spaces, particular built environments, paintings, museums, and the like that imagine new meanings or possibilities for spatial practices'.[9]It is thus interesting to note that the present Kamtapur movement has emerged from the historical 'Kamta' or 'Koch Bihar' area of the northeast India. The area of the territory they are demanding for the proposed Kamtapur state is more or less as that of the old Kamta Kingdom, which was under the Koch dynasty. The Rajbongshi identify themselves with the princely state of Kamtapur or Kamta Kingdom. The memory of the Kamta kingdom works as the solo inspiration for the Koch Rajbongshi in Cooch Behar area who wish to restore the glory of old Kamta Kingdom and of the Rajbongshi. The merger of Cooch Behar state with the West Bengal and its transformation from a native state to a mere district of West Bengal thus plays a very important role in triggering the present Kamtapur Movement. [10] Cooch Behar never formed a part of Bengal before the advent of the British rule in India.[11] Accordingly the leadership of the Kamtapur Movement demand a separate state of Kamtapur on historical grounds that Cooch Behar and the adjoining areas were never a part of the West Bengal and are composed of ethnic groups with culture and language totally distinct from that of West Bengal.

Like every modern state West Bengal too is marked by cultural diversity with the presence of different cultural communities seeking preservation of their distinct culture. Cultural diversity as emanating from the indigenous peoples or the 'original nations' is predominant in West Bengal. The 'original nations' as termed by Parekh seek to preserve their distinct ways of life which is integrally bound up with land which they lost to colonizers. Although they once enjoyed independence which they later lost to white colonizers, they do not generally seek to form themselves into independent states. Rather their primary aim is to recover or retain their land and be given the autonomy to lead their traditional ways of life within the framework of the existing states. This form of cultural diversity emanating from the indigenous peoples or the 'original nations' in West Bengal reflects the case of Koch Rajbongshi who lost their princely state of 'Cooch Behar' to the British colonisers and were later integrated into the state of West Bengal through Instrument of Accession. Koch Rajbongshi now seeks to recover or retain their land in the form of a separate state of Kamtapur. They do not demand secession from India but a separate state within the Indian Union distinct from West Bengal.

Cultural Diversity in West Bengal: Threat From Within and Outside

The understanding of culture is driven with differences. This has led to the realization that cultures are not monolithic blocks that are oblivious of and neutral to considerations of power and politics. Cultures indeed express power relations, albeit in a veiled manner, and evoke emotions strong enough for people to die and kill for. It is true that cultures must communicate, but it is also true that this communication cannot presume a consensus, or a unified set of meanings. Culture is primarily practice in the pursuit of a 'good life'. The good life is not conceived individualistically or solipsistically. That cultural practice, as interaction, involves relations with other people. Minorities in a culturally diverse society often face challenge from the majoritarian community who oppose unravelling of the cultural character of the state that reflects the majoritarian cultural biases giving advantage to the majority communities over the minorities. Accordingly any attempt by the minority community to establish its claim in the majoritarian cultural structure is met with resistance by the majority community. This is visible even in the case of the Koch Rajbongshi as their demand for a separate state of Kamtapur has not been received well by the majority community of Bengalis in West Bengal.

There is no similarity in thought, perception as well as socio-political behaviour between majoritarian community that is the Bengalis and the minority ethnic communities of Rajbongshi who form a dominant settlement in the geographical areas of Cooch Behar in West Bengal. The Rajbongshi profess and follow language, culture, tradition, social rites entirely different to the rest of West Bengal. According to Kymlicka, indigenous people as national minorities resist state nation-building policies and instead fight for some form of territorial self-government. They offer justifications for doing so by appealing to their unjust incorporation into the state and the central importance of their land, language and culture to their identity and autonomy. Indigenous communities challenge state authority and seek autonomy to assert and restore the status that they once had as separate Nations within the polity and it is in this capacity that they seek these rights. One can thus say that though the historical background is not the sole criteria for the creation of a separate state, it of course forms an important factor in any such demands.

The number of lawmakers a state can send to the Indian Parliament depends on its population and a state's bargaining power in a federal coalition government. Such electoral calculations determine how both the federal and state governments respond to popular demands. The asymmetry in population ensures that more federal and state funding flows to the more populated regions and the majority community. In the West Bengal state assembly, which has 294 legislators, Cooch Behar sends a mere three members respectively. Rajbongshi as an ethnic minority in West Bengal lack adequate political representation in the governmental machinery. The total strength of MPs and MLAs representing the Rajbongshi is insufficient in relation to area and growing population since the inception of the West Bengal Legislative Assembly.

Conflicts between linguistic groups because of economic discrimination are not an uncommon phenomenon. Identities based on language become politically volatile when the ruling class and the subjugated belong to different linguistic communities. For instance in Canada, the Quebecois resented the economic and political domination of Anglophone in Quebec but expressed it in terms of the confrontation between French and English languages. The concerted attempts of the Quebecois in the late seventies to give Quebec a French visage was largely a response to the economic domination by the English in the region. The emphasis on French as the primary language in Quebec brought about a change in the nature of social interactions as the social background of personnel also changed from French to English. Those who were earlier linguistically handicapped now became linguistically privileged. To take an example from India, the hostility against the English language from sections of Hindu nationalists was on account of the social prestige that was attached to English even after independence from British rule. Undermining the role of English language from public life brought people of lower middle class and of rural backgrounds to greater prominence. This had a profound effect on the nature of social relations as new ambitions were stoked while older styles of civil service leadership and rule became ineffectual.

Accordingly the Rajbongshi have formed the opinion that the culture and the history of the Rajbongshi is neither recognised nor promoted by the West Bengal Government. The Rajbongshi heroes and history are not glorified in West Bengal in spite of the legendary history as Arnold Toynbee said that there are three heroes in history: Chilarai (Rajbongshi legend), Bonaparte and Napolean.[12] Even the Lal Kothi in Darjeeling was the residing place of the royals of the princely state of Cooch Behar which is now the GTA office. Moreover the Rajbongshi Academy established by West Bengal Government is a namesake organisation and does not promote the culture of the Rajbongshi. Even the Cooch Behar State Library has been renamed as North Bengal State Library to deny Cooch Behar recognition and relevance (see image below). The Kamtapuri language, culture and practices although is totally different from Bengalis of West Bengal, the majority community deny the Rajbongshi to be different from Bengalis and consider it to be a part of the broader culture of the Bengalis. This is mainly because of the fear that if they glorify the history and culture of the Rajbongshi it would overshadow the history, culture and language of the Bengalis itself.

Figure 2: North Bengal State Library, Coochbehar

Immigration has further generated challenges for the ethnic minorities in West Bengal as cross border migration from Bangladesh continues to remain unchecked mired with the compulsions of electoral politics. The Rajbongshi in West Bengal do not view cross border migration from Bangladesh as a threat to their distinct identity. However they express discontent over the resultant economic setback as their land and jobs are passed away either to the Bangladeshis or Bengalis from South Bengal. Even the exchange of enclaves between Bangladesh and India was apprehended to cause large scale migration of people from Bangladesh to India which would then turn Rajbongshi into minorities in areas now dominated by them. The subsequent alienation from their ancestral land and the transformation of Rajbongshi from land owning peasants to wage labour class and the land acquisition by the immigrants has resulted into cornering of the Rajbongshi people in West Bengal. The Kamtapur movement is thus an ultimate outcome of the struggle for power and the associated privileges between the indigenous communities (particularly the Rajbongshi) on one hand and the Bengali migrants as well as Bangladeshi immigrants on the other. It exemplifies the efforts of an indigenous commu-nity in putting up a resistance to their gradual economic marginalisation and erosion of cultural and linguistic identity due to cross border immigration.[13]

According to the Rajbongshi ethnic community of West Bengal, Cooch Behar in spite of a monarchical rule was a model in the whole of the Indian sub-continent in the first half of the twentieth century in terms of education, agro-based industry and agriculture sector. However with the merger of Cooch Behar with the state of West Bengal it is decaying and lagging behind most other districts of the southern Delta of West Bengal. The rural areas are in skeletal shapes of economic resources. Thousands of jobless people are migrating to other states in search of means of livelihood. This has resulted into mounting frustration owing to the dispossession of their earlier self-sufficient way of life leading to emotional outburst against the government and people in power by the Rajbongshi in West Bengal. [14]

Vernacular Identity Politics and Rajbongshis in West Bengal

Pride in language among ethnic communities generally emanates from the relative feelings of superiority in their language. Such a feeling is derived from a similar feeling of superiority in their caste, religion, kinship, etc, that dominate the interaction which takes place among speakers of a particular language. Membership based on language as such can intersect with other memberships based on caste or religion. For instance, in 1905 when Bengal was proposed to be partitioned by the British, there was an all-Bengal agitation against it. This agitation brought together Bengalis irrespective of religion and caste. In the agitation against the British partition of Bengal religion became a major divisive force, strong enough to negate the bonds of language. In contrast the agitation for the independence of East Pakistan later known as Bangladesh was made on the grounds of language. In spite of overlapping memberships, it is often the historic experience that one kind of membership is sometimes put above all others. Such a phenomenon is also visible in the case of the Koch Rajbansi in West Bengal. Their identity politics that germinated as a caste movement culminated into a linguistic movement demanding recognition of Kamtapuri language in the eighth schedule of the Indian Constitution. Linguistic is now clearly being held above the caste identity. Linguistic membership is thus sublimated phenomenon as pointed by Dipankar Gupta who further opined that on occasions a membership may be denied altogether by self-consciously repudiating an identity that was earlier held in common. The Kshatriya Movement of the Koch Rajbongshi that held in common the identity of Kshatriya by the Koch Rajbongshi faded into oblivion as demands were made to be recognised as Schedule Caste community to reap the benefits of protective discrimination.

As a response to the volatile Gorkhaland Movement led by Subhash Ghisingh in 1980s Nepali language was recognized by the State Government of West Bengal in 1961 as an official language in the state. However the inclusion of the 'Kamtapuri' language in the Eighth Schedule of the Indian Constitution still remains a desire unfulfilled of the Rajbongshi. The KPP failed to project the language issue with the necessary force of argument, although they insisted on recording their language as Kamtapuri in the census. In view of this, the state started the campaign that Kamtapuri was not a language but a dialect of the Bengali language and desisted people from recording it as their mother tongue. Several public meetings were held with linguistics from Kolkata to drive home their argument. This triggered off the emotion and anger of the Rajbongshi intellectuals who responded by holding meetings and seminars and denounced the state campaign against the Kamtapuri language as cultural colonialism. The Rajbongshi insisted that the Kamtapuri from earlier times is an autonomous language of Rajbongshi community living within the Kamta culture. The Rajbongshi is not the sub caste of Bengalis and Rajbongshi language not the sub-language of the Bengali as claimed by the dominant community in West Bengal.[15] According to them, Kamtapuri is a different language having particular traits of its own. They insist that the Rajbongshi language is the originator of the Sanskrit language for every word of the Rajbongshi has the pronunciation of 'Om' in it making it one of the oldest language in the civilization.[16] Thus all other language including Bengali, Poliya and Desias originated from the Rajbongshi language. The Rajbongshi are inclined to the idea that the Bengali language has been imposed upon them, and the very existence of their culture is threatened by Bengali chauvinistic aggression. With the background of linguistic state formation in India, the Rajbongshi struggle to prove Kamtapuri as a separate language to strengthen their claim for a separate state Kamtapuri along linguistic lines.

With regard to the language demand of the KPP, the CPI (M) government of West Bengal from 1977-2011 asserted that the Kamtapuri language is only a dialect of the Bengali language and hence denied it an official status in West Bengal. The government of West Bengal held several public meetings with linguistics from the capital campaigning that Kamtapuri was not a language but a dialect of the Bengali language and desisted people from recording it as their mother tongue. It held that many colloquial languages have contributed to the development of the Bengali language including the Kamtapuri which remained a dialect of the local ethnic people.[17] KPP however has been able to enlist the support of several organisations that operate in the region like the CPI (ML) Santosh Rana faction, CPRM, Samajwadi Jana Parishad, Uttar Bengal Jharkhandi Sangarsh Samiti, etc for its demand for the recognition of the Kamtapuri language in the Eighth Schedule of the Indian Constitution. Though all these organisations do not support the demand for a separate state; some of these organisations endorsed the claim of the KPP for the recognition of the Kamtapuri language to be one of the official languages of West Bengal.

The KPP leadership associated with the Trinamool Congress (TMC) in 2001 with KPP president Atul Roy saying that, "Mamata Banerjee's aim is to banish the CPI (M); we also hold the same view. As such we need to have an alliance with Mamata". However the Mamata Banerjee-led TMC alliance with the Kamtapur People's Party was routed in the very districts that had cradled the movement. Encouraged by the Rajbongshi party's failure, the Left Front government, in 2003, ordered a crackdown that crushed the KLO and landed its leaders in jail. In 2012, in response to the GCPA revival of the separate statehood movement Mamata Banerjee who was by then the Chief Minister of West Bengal established the Rajbongshi Bhasha Academy as a compensatory gesture. Looking for a toehold in West Bengal, the BJP had then readily promised to fulfil the Rajbongshis' demand for statehood and a distinct linguistic identity. The GCPA also saw the BJP's stated position on Gorkhaland as a sign of its sincerity and consequenty the Rajbongshi community voted for the BJP in 2014. Mamata's numerous attempts to placate ethnic sentiments in West Bengal clearly did not work, as the 2016 by-elections in Cooch Behar showed. The BJP had cornered an impressive vote share of 28 per cent in the polls with approximately 150,000 new voters. Under the circumstances, the ruling TMC in a bid to woo north Bengal's ten million Rajbongshi, who voted for the BJP in the 2014 Lok Sabha elections, on February 28th, 2018 recognised the Rajbongshi dialect, alongside Kamtapuri and Kurmali, as an official language.[18]

The West Bengal Legislative Assembly passed the West Bengal Official Language (Second Amendment) Bill, 2018 moved by States Parliamentary Affairs and Education Minister Partha Chatterjee was passed by voice vote. Chief Minister Mamata Banerjee said that the decision to include the three languages in the official languages list was based on the recommendation by a seven-member Expert Committee headed by scholar Nrisingha Prasad Bhaduri. Ruling out the allegation made by the opposition CPI (M) and Congress that recognition to Kamtapuri language would instigate their separatist movement Chief Minister Mamata Banerjee insisted that an amendment to the West Bengal Official Languages Act, 1961 was necessary to declare these three local languages as official languages in the district, sub-division, block or municipality, where the population of Kamtapuri or

Rajbongshi or Kurmali speaking people exceeded ten per cent as a whole or part of the district like sub-division or block.[19] Chief Minister Mamata Banerjee further formed the Rajbongshi Development and Cultural Board on June 7th, 2017 and Kamtapuri Bhasa Academy on September 13th, 2017 with the objective to ensure all round development of the Rajbongshis. Bangshi Badan Barman who has been leading the Greater Cooch Behar movement was made the vice-chairman of the Rajbongshi Bhasa Academy. However he insisted that the agitation for the separate state will continue and that it has nothing to do with this board.[20]

A large section of the Rajbongshi-Koch community strongly argued that this language should be termed as Rajbongshi language. Most of them argued that the Rajbongshi and Koches are same and by naming the language as Rajbongshi, the psychological division if any among the Rajbongshi community will be eliminated. Dr. Grierson also called it Rajbongshi dialect. While an interview was taken, Dr. Giraja Shankar Roy, ex-principal of a college and author of several books, belonged to the Rajbongshi community strongly supported the name Rajbongshi language. The other school of thought strongly opposed it. Dharmanarayan Burman, ex head master belonged to the Rajbongshi community and consider that Rajbongshi and the Koch are different in their origin and as such they are not identical, argued at, Rajbongshi language is not only the court language of the Rajbongshi King but it was also the court language of the Koch kingdom and this was more developed in the hand of the Koch kings. It was/is the mother tongue of Muslims, Rajbongshis, Kayasthas, Brahmins, Khens, and other people of old Kamtapuri kingdom. So in his opinion the language should be called Kamta-Bihari'language.[21]

The second "bhasa" academy was also necessitated in view of the differences within the community over whether the language should be called Rajbongshi or Kamtapuri. To prevent any confusion or differences, the state decided to float another academy for the language called Kamtapuri Bhasa Academy with Atul Roy who is also the chairman of the Kamtapur Progressive Party as the vice-chairman was formed on. The offices of the Rajbongshi Development and Cultural Board and the Rajbongshi Bhasa Academy would be in Cooch Behar, while the Kamtapuri Bhasa Academy would be headquartered in Jalpaiguri. The government is moving towards introducing Kamtapuri language at primary level in schools. The work for a grammar book for the language is in progress. The moves are being seen as a part of Chief Minister Mamata Banerjee's strategy to gain the confidence of the Rajbongshis who were of late seen to be courting the BJP.[22]

Kamtapur Movement and State Apathy

The idea for a separate homeland for the Koch Rajbongshi has been spearheaded by various organizations in West Bengal. Uttarkhand Dal (UKD) demanded the formation of the Kamtapur State in 1969, but did not make much political headway and was first replaced by the Kamtapur Gana Parishad in 1987, to be followed by Kamtapur Peoples' Party (KPP) in 1997. At present, it is the KPP which is a North Bengal based political organization, which is spearheading the demand for separate Kamtapur state for the Koch Rajbongshi community. KPP's demand is only statehood, not sovereignty. Besides statehood, KPP is also demanding the inclusion of the Kamtapuri or Rajbongshi language in the Eighth Schedule and the propagation of the Kamtapuri language and culture through the state controlled radio and television. However the Kamtapur Movement marred by split in Kamtapur People's Party owing to ideological and political difference failed to emerge as an effective and organized ethno-autonomy movement in West Bengal. Consequently the West Bengal government considered the Kamtapur movement as merely a law and order situation showing political apathy towards the same. For long the CPI (M) led government by Chief Minister Buddhadeb Bhattacharjee refused to even hold talks with the KPP leaders.

With regard to the movement for a separate state by Rajbongshi the Govt of West Bengal led by Left Front used two different strategies to counter the Kamtapur Movement. First, it used strong-arm tactics, and second, it concentrated on the economic development of the region. The first strategy included the use of police force in order to counter the mobilisation by the KPP/GCPA. The government of West Bengal alleges that the KPP has links with the KLO and that it is the militant wing of the later. 'Operation Kamtapur' as such was launched by the West Bengal government in November 2000 to counter the terrorist activities of the KLO.[23] However the CPI (M)-led Left Front government in West Bengal took up a programme to rehabilitate the surrendered militants of KLO. Five such militants, including Madhusudan Das, who had surrendered following former Chief Minister Buddhadeb Bhattacharjee's appeal were reported to have been given Rs.12,000 each and the license to start trade in river bed materials.[24] The second strategy included greater funds for the region. The government of West Bengal attempted to uplift the economic plight of the Rajbongshi populace by implementing various policies such as Rural Development Schemes, Welfare Scheme for SC and ST, etc. The government of West Bengal also constituted a developmental agency, i.e., the Uttarbanga Unnagan Parshad especially to remove the economic backwardness of Cooch Behar.

However the development policies pursued by the governments in West Bengal failed to alter the economic backwardness of Cooch Behar and so the economic condition of the Rajbongshi. According to the West Bengal Human Development Report (2004), the rate of the rural poverty in the central districts of Jalpaiguri and Cooch Behar was as high as 35.73 and 25.62 per cent respectively. Incidentally, these are the two districts which have high concentration of Rajbongshi. Atul Roy, President of KPP in an interview published in The Week, November 16th, 2003 opined that the economic condition of the Rajbongshi in Cooch Behar has deteriorated tremendously during the 26 years of Left Front rule in West Bengal. Lack of irrigation facilities has reduced agriculture to a single crop a year. There has been no major development with regard to the Teesta Barrage Project launched by the Left Front government.[25] Even former Left Front leaders like Kamal Guha, belonging to the All India Forward Bloc, admitted that the region including Cooch Behar suffers from the problem of under development. To him, this was one of the reasons for the political and social unrest in the region. Buddhadev Bhattacharya, former Chief Minister of West Bengal conceded that dispossession of land and large-scale unemployment lie at the root of the grievances of the Rajbongshi populace in West Bengal. Similarly the CPI (ML) Liberation State Committee in West Bengal noted that the discontent and separatist sentiments of the Rajbongshi people is due to the continued neglect and deprivation of North Bengal. The West Bengal government led by the Communist Party thus viewed Kamtapur Movement as the desperate effort of the 'dispossessed landlords' to re-assert themselves as the dominant class in West Bengal.[26]

The present government of West Bengal considering the Kamtapur Movement as a law and order issue has spoken of stern action against the KLO after the Jalpaiguri blast (December 26th, 2013). The ruling Trinamool Congress Party led by Mamata Banerjee had also taken a public posture in early January, 2014 of confronting the KLO politically in 72 blocks where the latter is active. Though not in a denial mode on the backwardness of this community the state government have taken measures such as establishment of Cooch Behar Panchanan Barma University under the West Bengal Act XXI of 2012 and allocation of funds to Rajbongshi Development & Cultural Board to provide houses to poor Rajbongshi families living in the districts of Cooch Behar, Alipurduar, Jalpaiguri and Darjeeling. However the developmental schemes adopted appears to be inadequate with regard to the economic upliftment of the Rajbongshi who continue to remain backward and deprived.[27] The area inhabited by the Rajbongshi in North Bengal continues to be marked by underdevelopment owing to which they suffer from economic backwardness.

The separate state demand of the Greater Cooch Behar people Association (GCPA) has been criticized mainly by the Cooch Behar Zilla Left Front (CZLF). The members of the Zilla Left Front of Cooch Behar refute the 'C' category state demand of the GCPA on the ground that the Constitution through the 7th Amendment Act, 1995 substituted 'C' states with the category of 'Union Territories' which were to be similarly administered by the Union Government. Moreover the State Reorganisation Act, 1956 merged the part 'C' states of Ajmer, Bhopal, Coorg, Kutch and Vindhya Pradesh into other adjoining states. The Cooch Behar Zilla Left Front further argued that the 7th Amendment Act cancelled the status of Cooch Behar as a 'C' category state in the Indian Union in 1956. Accordingly Cooch Behar too like other states of Ajmer, Bhopal, Vindhya Pradesh, was attached with the adjoining state of West Bengal.[28] The CPI (M) also asserted that there was no demand for a separate state of Cooch Behar during the time of State Reorganisation Commission in 1956.

The West Bengal Government under the Left Front as well as Trinamool Congress too has denied support to the Kamtapur Movement. This is because the partition of Bengal for a second time is tantamount to losing vote bank in the whole of West Bengal dominated by the Bengali ethnic majority. Consequently no state level or national level political party extend support to the Rajbongshi demand for a separate state of Kamtapur. Moreover the Government on nationalistic considerations refrain from the very idea of a separate state of Cooch Behar for it would be a vulnerable state with sizeable Muslim population along the borders of Bangladesh, an Islamic state.[29] Thus consideration of GCPA's or KPPs demand for a separate state of Cooch Behar or Kamtapur respectively by the Union as well as the state government appears to be a far cry. In fact the West Bengal government view the Kamtapur Movement as unreasonable and unhistorical and condemns the activities of KPP and GCDP as terrorist and secessionist activities. Thus calling the Kamtapur Movement as a separatist movement, the West Bengal government vehemently opposes the demand of a separate state of Kamtapur.

Mainstream institutions in a culturally diverse society like that of West Bengal appear to privilege the majority's culture and identity in ways not intended. Suppression or exclusion of minority cultural practices in the public domain of the state is tantamount to cultural discrimination of the minorities. However by providing symbolic expression to the minority culture in the national symbols of the state, a step can be taken so as to protect their identities, make their cultures secure and give them a sense of recognition in the socio-political system. Attempts have therefore been made

Figure 3: Coochbehar Royal Palace now maintained by the Archaeological Survey of India

Figure 4: Statue of Rai Saheb Panchanan Barma in Siliguri, popularly known as 'Thakur Panchanan' by Koch Rajbangsi community in North Bengal.

by the Govt. of West Bengal to give equal recognition to the contribution of the Rajbongshis to the history and culture richness of the West Bengal. Maintenance of archaeological sites of the ethnic minorities by the Govt. of West Bengal exemplifies its attempts to accommodate cultural diversity in the national symbols of the state as seen in the images below:

A comparative analysis of the Kamtapur movement and Gorkhaland Movement in the district of Darjeeling of West Bengal one could help but notice that the state as well as the Union government has been more responsive to the Gorkhaland Movement in the hill districts of West Bengal than to the Kamtapur Movement. In response to the Gorkhaland Movement the union as well as the state government not only incorporated Nepali in the eight schedule of the Indian Constitution but also granted autonomous councils in the various stages of the Gorkhaland Movement. This could possibly be due to fact that the Gorkhaland Movement has been more organised and articulate in its statehood demand and strategies than the Kamtapur Movement. The violent mass uprising during the Gorkhaland Movement led by Subhash Ghising in the 1980s and the mass participation of the Gorkha populace in candle rallies during the present phase of the Gorkhaland Movement led by Bimal Gurung clearly illustrated that Gorkhas as an ethnic community are conscious and participative in their collective struggle for Gorkhaland. In contrast the socio-economic backwardness of the region of the Cooch Behar results into the lack of political consciousness and apathy among the Rajbongshi populace with regard to the Kamtapur movement. Moreover the Rajbongshi are not upfront and participatory on a mass level with regard to the Kamtapur movement which can also be the result of the alleged linkage of the KPP with the terrorist outfit KLO. The Rajbongshi intelligentsia also extends only passive support to the KPP. While they feel passionate about the plight of the Rajbongshi ethnic community in Cooch Behar they refrain from linking themselves to the organizations leading Kamtapur Movement. Owing to such display of political apathy and poor assertion of their demands on the part of the Rajbongshi, the KPP's efforts to exercise their collective bargaining power against the state have failed.

Kamtapur Movement: Saga of Reviving The Past Ethnic Glory

According to Dipankar Gupta historic agreements bring together nation-states that are not concentrated but dispersed and represent fault lines within nation-states. As a consequence it breeds ethnic and communal politics. Historic agreements therefore have to be supplanted over time and made redundant. The background and the necessity of the agreements have to be supplanted over time from popular consciousness and made redundant. However this requires skilful statesmanship which is usually in short supply. In the case of India the structure of the state emerged rather quickly after Independence. The dependence on the framework of the colonial state was immense as no serious thought was given to this aspect during the days of mobilization. As a result post independence there were several major political mobilizations launched on the basis of cultural identities. The demand of Koch Rajbongshi for a separate state of Kamtapur is also grounded in their history that can be traced to the 16th century Kamta kingdom which continued to remain a princely state under the British colonialism. The Cooch Behar province enjoyed the status of Chief Commissioners Province to be administered by the Chief Commissioner appointed by the British colonial government. Thus Cooch Behar was not brought under the rules of general administration existing in the larger parts of British colonial India. Post independence political situation in West Bengal underwent revolutionary change. Cooch Behar was merged with West Bengal in 1950 as a district against the will of local people of Cooch Behar. With the partition of Pakistan, there was a huge influx of refugees from East Bengal to the border districts of North Bengal pressurizing the land based rural economy. Moreover with the abolition of Privy Purse and Zamindari system by the Union Government led by Congress the major portion of landed property owned by the Rajbongshi jotedars were vested to the landless people belonging to both Rajbongshi and non-Rajbongshi ethnic groups. The merger of the princely state of Cooch Behar with the West Bengal also led to the influx of the Bengal nationals into the land of the Rajbongshi. The indigenous Rajbongshi populace subsequently lost their land to the affluent Bengalis with the implementation of the land ceiling acts enacted by the West Bengal government. This developed feelings of deprivation among the Rajbongshi landed aristocracy against the West Bengal government as its policy affected their economic interests.[30]

To conclude the under development of the Rajbongshi due to the loss of land and non-availability of employment opportunities culminated into feelings of alienation among the Rajbongshi. Consequently the Rajbongshi landed aristocracy mobilized the public opinion against the West Bengal government by drawing the attention of the Rajbongshi populace to the underdevelopment of the region. Eventually the neglect of the Rajbongshi dominated region by the West Bengal government gave rise to the demand for a separate state of Kamtapur mainly articulated by the Rajbongshi landed aristocracy.[31]The leaders of the Kamtapur movement considered merger of Cooch Behar with West Bengal as a conspiracy of West Bengal government and placed it as one of the main arguments in support of the demand for Kamtapur state. The misrule and negligence of the state and Union government towards Cooch Behar is also cited to be the reason behind the movement for a separate state of Kamtapur. Moreover, post Bangladesh liberation the Terai region of Darjeeling district as well as Cooch Behar was swamped by refugees from Bangladesh in an attempt to escape persecution. Immigration of the Bangladeshi nationals still continues in the region. This is perceived by the Rajbongshi to be a meticulous and systematised political move of the West Bengal government so as to weaken their claim for self government by gradually reducing them to a minority in their own traditional territory.

That Cooch Behar lags behind on developmental parameters described by various bodies is not contested by anyone. With low employment rates, poverty and immigration from Bangladesh, the region faces many challenges to grow along with other parts of the country. An afterglow of the glory days seen during the Kamtapur kingdom's reign still hangs around the Rajbongshis. The Rajbongshis believe that they are losing their ethnicity, culture and language owing to the majoritarian policies by the government. A lack of focused political action within the frameworks of democracy has further weakened the movement. Successful demands for statehood within India have been the result of mass movements on the ground where viable alternatives to the existing governance had been built. Sporadic protests gather attention but do not lead to action. The Kamtapur movement hence needs to emerge from the grassroots for it to gain ground and take it to its objective.

Notes

1. Arup Jyoti Das, Kamtapur and the Koch Rajbanshi Imagination, Montage Media Publication, Assam, India, 2009.
2. See Wbnorthbengaldev.gov.in.
3. Arabinda Deb, Bhutan and India: A Study in Frontier Political Relations (1772-1865), Firma KLM Private Limited, Calcutta, 1976, pp. 72-86.
4. Anirban Biswas, '*Destination Kamtapur*', Frontier, Volume 35 No 20, 2002, p.p. 9-10.
5. Arup Jyoti Das, Kamtapur and the Koch Rajbanshi Imagination , op.cit.no.1.
6. Anirban Biswas, '*Destination Kamtapur',* op.cit.no. 4.
7. Dipankar Gupta, Culture, Space and the Nation-State, Sage Publications, New Delhi, 2000, pp. 123.
8. Arup Jyoti Das, Kamtapur and the Koch Rajbanshi Imagination, Montage Media Publication, Assam, India, 2009, pp. 56.

9. Dipankar Gupta, Culture, Space and the Nation-State, Sage Publications, New Delhi, 2000, pp 105.
10. Ibid.
11. Arup Jyoti Das, Kamtapur and the Koch Rajbanshi Imagination, op.cit.no.1.
12. Girindra Narayan Ray, *The Rajbongshi Identity Politics: The Postcolonial Passages*, in Debnath Sailen, edited Social and Political Tensions in North Bengal (Since 1947), N.L. Publishers, Siliguri, West Bengal, 2007.
13. Moumita Ghosh Bhattacharyya, *Rajbanshis: The Deprived People of North Bengal (in the State of West Bengal,* International Journal of South Asian Studies, Volume 2 Number 2, Puducherry, July-December 2002.
14. Arup Jyoti Das, Kamtapur and the Koch Rajbanshi Imagination, op.cit.no.1.
15. Girindra Narayan Ray, '*The Rajbongshi Identity Politics: the postcolonial passages',* op.cit.no.12.
16. This is the opinion expressed by the General Secretary, The Greater Cooch Behar People's Association, Dinhata, Cooch Behar during the interview undertaken as part of the field work conducted for the present research.
17. See Girindra Narayan Ray, *'The Rajbanshi Identity Politics: The Post Colonia Passages'*, in Sailen Debnath, ed Social and Political Tensions in North Bengal (Since 1947), N.L. Publishers, Siliguri, West Bengal, 2007.
18. Romita Datta, '*West Bengal: Speaking their language'*, India Today, March 9, 2018. (www.indiatoday.in).
19. '*Kamtapuri, Rajbanshi make it to the list of official languages in the state'*, Press Trust of India wire, 28th February, 2018. (www.indiatoday.in).
20. '*CM announces formation of Rajbanshi Board',* Millennium Post, 12th September, 2017. (www.millenniumpost.in).
21. '*Ethno-linguistic aspects of the movement'* , chapter six, Shodhganga.(http://shodhganga.inflibnet.ac.in).
22. Avijit Sinha, '*Mamata creates new academy',* Telegraph, 13th September, 2017(https://www.telegraphindia.com).
23. Alok Kumar Gupta and Saswati Chanda, *'Kamptapur Liberation Organisation: The New Face of Terror'*, Third Concept, Volume XVI No. 191, January, 2003, pp. 56-58.
24. Suhrid Sankar Chattopadhyay, '*A Ruthless Hit Squad',* Frontline, Volume 21 - Issue 01, January 03 - 16, 2004.
25. Jaydeep Mitra, 'Lack of Development gives rise to Separatist Sentiments', http: //www.cpiml.org /liberation/year_2001/February/ 06%20special%20 report. Html.
26. See Ashutosh Kumar, Rethinking State Politics in India: Regions within Regions', Routledge, 2012, USA.
27. Gautam Sen, 'Need for action plan to counter KLO', Institute for Defence Studies and Analysis, February 28, 2014 (http: //www.idsa.in/idsacomments/Needfor actionplantocount erKLO gsen 280214).
28. Kamal Chandra Barman, *'Ethnic Movements in North Bengal: A Review of Kamtapur and Greater Cooch Behar State Demand in Cooch Behar'*, unpublished MPhil dissertation, University of North Bengal, 2007.

29. Anirban Biswas. '*Destination Kamtapur*', Frontier, Volume 35 Number 20, 2002, pp. 9-10.
30. Sukhbilas Barma, *'Social And Political Tension In North Bengal Since—1947'*, in Sailen Debnath ed Social and Political Tensions in North Bengal (Since 1947), N.L. Publishers, Siliguri, West Bengal, 2007.
31. Ashutosh Kumar, Rethinking State Politics in India: Regions Within Regions, op.cit. no. 27.

Chapter - VI

Conclusion

India since independence has made strides to politically accommodate the needs of its diversity. The Indian Constitution is reflective of the provisions that assure that the minorities are given special rights so as to recognize their cultural/religious uniqueness. Article 29(1) of the Indian Constitution says that any section of the citizens of India having a distinct language, script or culture of its own shall have the fundamental right to conserve the same. The Constitution also defines a positive, directional role for the state in this regard. It directs every state (federal units) to provide adequate facilities for instruction in the mother tongue at the primary stage of education of children belonging to linguistic minority groups. The Constitution not only provides for the protection of minority interests, but seeks to ensure that the individuals belonging to minorities do not suffer from discrimination. Article 29(2) forbids any discrimination against any citizen on the basis of religion, race caste or language in the matter of admission into educational institutions maintained or added by the state. As far as the institutional means of protection and cultivation of minority culture is concerned, Arts.29 (1) and 30(1) stipulate that the minorities can establish and administer educational institutions of their own choice, and the state cannot compel them to attend educational institutions not to their liking. However the aggrieved but territorially-rooted ethnic minorities find the existing provisions of the Constitution ineffective in protecting their identity within the existing state. Consequently they have taken recourse to statehood demands.[1] Various institutional measures such as the districts, or regional council, union territory, and associate states, or sub-state have been the state's response to such ethnic identity based statehood movements. Yet in many cases, the statehood movements have in fact grown out of dissatisfaction with the existing institutional measures as mentioned above.[2]

What needs to be understood is that people's identities are interwoven within their cultures, making cultures intrinsically worthy of respect. Cultural identity is quite important to ethnic communities and so they have a right to preserve their "way of life and the traits that are central identity components" for their culture. Because people's personality and way of life are so connected to their identity, people have a fundamental interest in maintaining their identity. To Margalit and Halbertal, "people who speak a particular language, for example, consider it important to preserve their language not because giving it up would mean giving up the use of language altogether, but because their culture is phrased in terms of the language, and they find particular linguistic treasures in it which they could not find in any other language". People's identity are partly constituted by the groups they are part of; since people's identity are part of who they are, and they have an interest in preserving this identity in some way, they have a justifiable interest in preserving their group.

Central to the ethno-identity movement is also a sense of alienation caused by some external force, which triggers autonomy movement by an ethnic community at the receiving end. These external forces may be a dominant ethnic group in the region, migrants from across the border or the Government reflecting the majoritarian biases unwilling to succumb to the demands of autonomy so as to maintain its zone of authority. In the case of Rajbongshi in West Bengal it was all the above external forces that posed threat to their distinct ethnic identity. Kamtapur Movement is marked by the desire to establish the identity of the Rajbongshi as a separate ethnic community distinctive from the majoritarian culture of the Bengalis in West Bengal. The fear of assimilation into the majoritarian culture and losing their distinctive ethnic identity is foremost among the Rajbongshi as they hold immense pride and conviction in their rich unique history, traditions, language and practices. They detest any claim made by the majoritarian Bengali ethnic community that Rajbongshi form a part of the larger Bengali ethnic culture. Instead they trace the history of the Rajbongshi settlement to ancient Kamta Kingdom in 16th century. They insist that the culture of the Rajbongshi is much older than the dominant culture of Bengalis in West Bengal and that the Bengali as a language emerged from the ancient Kamtapuri language. The inspiration for the present Kamtapur movement thus has been drawn from the historical Kamtapur or Kamta Kingdom, which became a princely state of British India in the 18th century and later merged into West Bengal as a district post-independence. In addition to this, the fear that the Bangladeshis patronized by various political parties for the sake of vote bank will reduce the Rajbongshi into a minority ethnic group in their own land endangering their distinct ethnic identity has further deepened the feelings of ethnic unrest among the Rajbongshi. Accordingly the Rajbongshi view the separate state of Kamtapur as the only solution to their identity crisis. Rajbongshi as ethnic community believe that they have their own distinct culture, language, customs and traditional practices different from dominant ethnic community of Bengalis in West Bengal. As a result they find their inclusion within West Bengal as unjustified and unfair. Added to this is the alleged negligence of the region by the Government in planning its socio-economic development.

One cannot ignore the instrumental aspects of Kamtapur Movement as well. The much needed development of Cooch Behar has come to a standstill as no effective attempts to further enhance or even maintain its infrastructural facilities were made. This has largely affected the local population in Cooch Behar as tea and cinchona plantation which are income generating units suffered a setback due to low productivity, marketing mismanagement, inadequate technical training to the workers and bankruptcy. This has led to the closure of many such plantations rendering the workers jobless. The administration failed to provide even the basic amenities like proper roads and adequate water supply to the people in Cooch Behar. It failed to harness the economic potentialities of the region which is rich in biodiversity and geographical features. Thus in the absence of an effective implementation of a viable economic strategy a sense of socio-economic deprivation started brewing in the plains of Cooch Behar erupting into the renewed movement for separate statehood in West Bengal.

Politically too, the administration proved to be inefficient as the West Bengal Government kept itself aloof from the political developments in the plains of Cooch Behar. Kamtapur movement as such has also emerged out of the desire for self governance. The desire to have the power to frame their own policies has led to the movement for separate statehood in West Bengal. The right to governance is viewed as the political right by the ethnic minorities like the Rajbongshi who want to get out of the Bengal political dominance so as to frame all the policies for a region with different culture, history, language and tradition. They demand true decentralization of power in the form of separate statehood. Besides apathy of Government with regard to the history, cultural practices and language of the Rajbongshi ethnic minorities further deepened feelings of alienation among them. The ethnic culture and language of the Rajbongshi for a long time was refuted by the Government to be distinct from the larger Bengali culture in West Bengal. It was largely seen to be the very part of the Bengali culture with no ethnic individuality whatsoever. Rajbongshi culture as such has been denied recognition as even their language continues to be bereft of Eighth Schedule status although Chief Minister Mamata Banerjee included Rajbongshi and

Kamtapuri in the West Bengal official languages list in 2018. The majoritarian Bengali community on the other hand through organizations like Amra Bengali and Bangla O Bangla Bhasha Banchao Committee has time and again expressed their protest against any dialogue or discussion between the Government and the ethnic minorities on their demand for separate statehood. They have openly condemned the idea of the further partition of Bengal as a means to accommodate the demands of the ethnic minorities in West Bengal. Accordingly accommodation of the interests of the ethnic minorities against those of the majoritarian community is no less a challenge to the harmonious cultural diversity in West Bengal.

Under such circumstances one is confronted with the questions as to how to accommodate ethno cultural differences and avoid exclusion of the members of minority groups. One way to remedy ethno cultural differences is through minority rights. Will Kymlicka in his ideas on minority rights identified two sources of cultural diversity. First, the involuntary incorporation of different culture into a single state through invasion or colonisation where one cultural community is invaded and conquered by another, or is ceded from one imperial power to another. Such a state is termed by Kymlicka as 'Multination' states which can also arise voluntary if different cultures mutually agree to form a federation for their mutual benefit. Second, when a country accepts immigrant families and individuals from cultures distinct from its own it results into cultural diversity. Kymlicka termed it 'Polyethnic' state which allows the immigrants to maintain their ethnic distinctions and attempts to bring about their institutional integration. Kymlicka further defends 'group-specific rights' on the ground that they are rights of non-discrimination. Kymlicka distinguishes between national minorities and the ethnic minorities on the ground that the while the former are indigenous people occupying homelands the latter are immigrants that do not occupy homelands. Kymlicka clearly underlines that the self government rights is meant for the national minorities while poly ethnic rights are for the ethnic minorities. In order to ensure the integration of the ethnic minorities in the host society their right to preserve and practice their culture is rightly promoted by the Kylimka in the form of poly ethnic rights. However categorising minorities into indigenous peoples, national minorities, and immigrant groups on the lines of Western models of cultural diversity and minority rights have limitation when applied to the case of Rajbongshi in West Bengal.

The demand of the Rajbongshi for self-government can be justified as the one by the national minorities with the desire to preserve and maintain their unique culture as distinct from the majoritarian community of West

Bengal. While the Rajbongshi clearly fit in the category of national minorities the self government right as suggested by Kymlicka involving federalism, require that the boundaries of the federal subunits be redrawn to ensure that the national minority forms a majority in one of the subunits. If this is effected this may empower Rajbongshi to make its own decisions without the fear of being outvoted by the majority. However redrawing of the boundaries of the federal subunits has the potential to unravel the territorial integrity of not just West Bengal but also Assam as the Rajbongshi form a majority not only in the Cooch Behar district of West Bengal but also in the neighbouring districts of Assam. Special representative rights in the form of proportional representation have been granted to the Rajbongshi. It however falls short to provide adequate representation of Koch Rajbongshis in the legislature and governmental agencies as ethnic minority. Accordingly reservation of seats could be an effective means to ensure greater share of the Rajbongshi in the political institutions of the state.

The Kamtapur Movement in Cooch Behar district of West Bengal is mainly founded on ethnicity which centres on common history, culture, tradition, language and social practices shared by the Rajbongshi in India. The desire of the Rajbongshi to preserve their distinctive identity as against the Bengalese in West Bengal led to the drive for personal identity based on primordial ties. As 'Primordialism' is essentially a question of emotion or affect, the Rajbongshi identity issue and the Kamtapur Movement can be studied from the perspective of primordialist theory since the Movement has a strong emotional basis. Apart from this, the development of the movement also clearly underlines the use ethnicity as political resource as not unoften the political entrepreneurs manipulate ethnic symbols for gaining the support of the masses in order to achieve their own individual political goals. This was clearly established in case of Kamtapur Movement during the 1980s when KPP appealed to the lost identity of the Rajbongshi so as to meet their political aspirations.

The West Bengal state has made strides to maintain cultural diversity by providing symbolic recognition to the ethnic minority culture in its national heritage. However mere symbolic recognition in the form of naming of street or building of statues of heroes of ethnic minorities falls short to eliminate feelings of alienation among the ethnic minorities. This is mainly because the territorially-rooted ethnic minorities desire respectful recognition and acceptance of their unique identity through the means of decentralization of power and autonomy to decide their own affairs. This in turn is possible only when they have an adequate share in the decision making process. Accordingly the Rajbongshi ethnic minorities demand not merely the symbolic representation of their ethnic culture. Instead they demand separate state for the protection of their ethnic identity as well as development. Decision making process in West Bengal should thus be inclusive that brings together Rajbongshi ethnic minorities particularly on matters pertaining to their welfare. It is to be ensured that their voice is not lost amidst the clamour of the majoritarian community. Equal civil, political, economic rights are to be also accompanied with cultural rights. However while the state grants to its citizens all these rights it fails to create an appropriate conditions for one to enjoy these rights. Ethnic minorities like Rajbongshi can fully enjoy their cultural rights as guaranteed by the Constitution of India when their distinctive culture is given due recognition and respect together with a sense of security in public and private realm.

To sum up the strength of a democracy lies in the hands of the people. The beauty of India's rich cultural heritage lies within our tolerant and protective stance towards our minorities. It is this inherent nature that has fuelled our growth, our pride and has been a shining beacon of unity in diversity. Our Constitution recognizes this and protects our rights, provides us a framework to determine our future while safeguarding our past. Inclusive growth has been the goal of our founders and leaders across history. While cultures evolve with time and grow, it is our duty to not force change upon people. Unwanted change leads to discontent, resentment and a sense of mistrust amongst people. The Rajbongshis have had a glorious past of the Kamtapur kingdom, but are unable to see a bright future for them. Lack of opportunity, development, years of neglect have seen them looking at the administration with forlorn eyes. With immigrants who bring with them their own distinctive culture thriving on their lands have made them see over time their indigenous Rajbongshi culture and language being slowly fading away. What was once a matter of pride is now only lived through grandma's tales at night. The Rajbongshis seek to revive some of the old glory, give their language a fresh lease of life and have the freedom of self administration as a state or union territory within India. The Kamtapur movement however lacks the leadership, mass mobilization and vigour that other successful statehood campaigns have seen. It is perhaps not wrong to say that what was once a fiery movement is now reduced to embers. Whether these embers light up again or die away slowly in an agonizingly long night for the Rajbongshis, only time can tell.

Notes

1. Harihar Bhattacharyya, *'Multiculturalism, Autonomy for Ethno-National Groups and the Unity of India'*, in edited Multiculturalism: Public Policy and Problem

Areas in Canada and India, Christopher Raj, Marie Mc Andrews, Jawaharlal Nehru University, New Delhi, 2009.

2. Gurpreet Mahajan , *'Negotiating Cultural Diversity and Minority Rights in India',* Democracy, Conflict and Human Security: Further Readings, Centre for Political Studies, Jawaharlal Nehru University, New Delhi, India.

Select Bibliography

1. Acharya S.K, *'Ethnic Processes in North-Eastern India'*, Economic and Political Weekly, Volume.23, No.21, May 21, 1988.
2. Brass Paul, Ethnicity and Nationalism- Theory and Comparison, Sage Publication, New Delhi, 1991.
3. Bhattacharya S S, *Uttarakhand Movement: A Sociological Analysis*, Special Lecture VIII, Centre for Himalayan Studies, University of North Bengal, West Bengal, 27th February, 1987.
4. Biswas Anirban, *Destination Kamtapur*, Frontier, Volume 35 No.20, 2002.
5. Craig Calhoun, *'Nationalism and Ethnicity'*, Annual Review of Sociology, Volume.19, 1993.
6. Chattopadhyay Suhrid Sankar, *A Ruthless hit squad*, Frontline, Volume 21 No.1, 2004.
7. Das Gurudas, 'Migration, *Ethnicity and Competition for State Resources'*, in (Ed) Northeast India – The Human Interface, (Eds M.K. Raha and Aloke Kumar Ghosh), Gyan Publications, New Delhi.
8. Deb Arabinda, Bhutan and India: A Study in Frontier Political Relations (1772-1865), Firma KLM Private Limited, Calcutta, 1976.
9. Das Arup Jyoti, Kamatapur and the Koch Rajbanshi Imagination, Montage Media Publication, Assam, India, 2009.
10. Dasgupta Rajarshi, *'The CPI (M) Machinery in West Bengal: Two Village Narratives from Kochbihar and Malda'*, Economic and Political Weekly, Volume XLIV No 9, February 28, 2009.
11. Debnath Sailen, edited Social and Political Tensions in North Bengal (Since 1947), N.L. Publishers, Siliguri, West Bengal, 2007.
12. ——————, The Dooars in Historical Transition, N.L. Publishers, Siliguri, West Bengal, 2010.
13. Eagleton Terry, The Idea of Culture, Blackwell Publishers, Great Britain, 2000.

14. Gupta Dipankar, Culture, Space and the Nation-State, Sage Publications, New Delhi, 2000.

15. Gupta Jyotirindra Das, '*Nation, Region, and Welfare: Ethnicity, Regionalism, and Development Politics in South Asia',* Annals of the American Academy of Political and Social Science, Volume. 433, May 21, 2007.

16. Gupta Alok Kumar and Saswati Chanda, *Kamptapur Liberation Organisation: The New Face of Terror*, Third Concept, Volume XVI No. 191, January 2003.

17. Hutchinson John and Anthony Smith (Ed.), Ethnicity, Oxford University Press, New York, 1996.

18. Hussain Monirul, *'State, Identity Movements and Internal Displacement in the North- east'*, Economic and Political Weekly, Volume 35, No 51, December 16, 2000.

19. Jenkins Richard, Rethinking Ethnicity, Sage Publications, New Delhi, 2008.

20. Majeed Akhtar, *'The Changing Politics of State's Re-organization'*, The Journal of Federalism, 2003.

21. Mukhopadhyay Rajat Subhra, *Contradiction and change in social identity of the Rajbansis,* Journal of the Indian Anthropological Society, Volume 34 No. 2, July 1999.

22. ————————————, *Kshatriyaization Among the Rajbansi: An Appraisal*, Man in India, Volume 79 No.3 & 4, July-December, 1999.

23. ————————————-, *Language movements: some issues and problems*, Journal of the Anthropological Survey of India, Volume 50 No. 1-2; March-June 2001.

24. ————————————, *Social Formation of the Rajbangsi and the Emergence of the Kamtapuri Identity,* edited Identity, Cultural Pluralism and the State: South Asia In Perspective, N K Das and V R Rao, Anthropological Survey of India, Macmillian Press, 2009.

25. Moumita Ghosh Bhattacharyya, *Rajbanshis: The Deprived People of North Bengal (in the State of West Bengal),* International Journal of South Asian Studies, Volume 2 Number 2, Puducherry,July-December 2002.

26. Nag Hiten, edited A History of Cooch Behar, N.L. Publishers, Siliguri, West Bengal, 2005.

27. Nath, D, *The Koches: their racial affinities and original homeland,* Journal of Indian History, Volume 64 No. 1-3, 1986

28. Nath D, *The Koches: Their Racial Affinities and Original Homeland*, Journal of Indian History, Volume 64 No.1-3, December 1986.

29. Patterson Orlando, *'what is ethnicity'*, Bulletin of the American Academy of Arts and Sciences, Volume. 27, No.8, May, 1974.

30. Phadnis Urmila and Rajat Ganguly, Ethnicity and Nation-Building in South Asia, Sage Publication, New Delhi, 2001.

31. Roy Sanjay K, *'Conflicting Nations in North-East India'*, Economic and Political Weekly, Volume.40, No.21, May 21, 2005.

32. Sarkar Dilip Kumar, *Integrated Decentralization: A Case of Cooch Behar District in West Bengal*, Journal of Indian Anthropology, Volume XXV No.2, January-December, 1998.

33. Sharma Shagun, *'Exploring the Different Meanings of Autonomy'*, Mainstream, Volume 46, No.25, June 8, 2008.

34. Smith Anthony D, *'Culture, Community and Territory: The Politics of Ethnicity and Nationalism'*, Ethnicity and International Relations (Royal Institute of International Affairs, 1994), Volume.72, No. 3, July 1996.

35. —————————— *'The Resurgence of Nationalism? Myth and Memory in the Renewal of Nations'*, The British Journal of Sociology, Volume. 47, No. 4, December 1996.

36. Varshney Ashutosh, *'Ethnicity and Ethnic conflict'*, in (Ed) The Oxford Handbook of Comparative Politics, (Eds Carles Boix and Susan C. Stokes), July 2009.

Annexures

GREATER COOCH BEHAR DEMOCRATIC PARTY

(G.C.D.P)

Head Office :- Prantik Bazar, Dinhata, Cooch Behar

President: Ashutosh Barma
Vill: Keshari Bari
P.O. Dhumer Khata, Sitai
Cooch Behar (M- 9932649865)

G. Secretary
P.N. Barman
M- 9733066712

Ref No. GCDP/121/09

Date:- 7.1.2009

To
Her Excellency President of India
Rastrapati Bhawan
New Delhi.

Through The B.D.O
Mathabhanga Block No. II

Sub :-- Prayer to declare Cooch Behar as a state Under union of India with a view to save the ethnic people of Cooch Behar ; as Cooch Behar was recognized as a state in the constitution of India on 26 th November, 1949.

Respected Madam ,

With due respect I on behalf of the Greater Cooch Behar Democratic party as well as the people of Cooch Behar have the honour to inform you , that we have informed about the matter to His Excellency President of India , the Hon'ble Prime Minister of India and hon'ble Home Minister of india vide our Petitions dated on 4th July 1995 to up date that the merger of the then Cooch Behar State with West Bengal on 1st January 1950 by Dr. Bidhan Chandra Roy the then Chief minister of West Bengal is fully illegal , un constitutional and initially void and the people of Cooch Behar State raised their voice against this illegal merger.

That sir, I beg to inform you that before British rule in India, Maharaja Naranarayan of Cooch Behar conquired all the small state of North Eastern India in 16th century and defended the North Eastern Border of India from foreign aggression in dignified way and Protected all the small states of North Eastern India under the territory of India . The State of Cooch Behar was known in 16th century as Kamtapur State . During British rule in India some areas of this state was occupied tactfully by the East India Company in 1773 A.D. India became free from British rule on 15 th August 1947 and a National Govt was formed in India Pandit Jawharlal Nehru the then Prime Minister . Sandar Vallabhvai Patel the then Home Minister of India requested the Kings of all native states of India to merge their states with union of India to make India as a powerful sovereign state in Asia. On the basis of such request of the Govt. of India Sir Jagaddipendra Narayan Bhup Bahadur the

RECEIVED
Contents not verified
Dealing Assistant
A.D.O's Office

then Maharaja of Cooch Behar discussed with them regarding the proper Status of Cooch Behar state and it's people with union of India. Pandit Nehru and Patel on behalf of the Govt. of India fully assured the Maharaja of Cooch Behar that they decided to keep Cooch Behar as a state with union of India in dignified way as the people of Cooch Behar may solve their various Political , economical and other problems in prompt manner . On the basis of such discussion and assurance of the Govt. of India Maharaja of Cooch Behar state signed a special agreement with government of India on 20th of August, 1948 for the accession of Cooch Behar to central administration .On the basis of this historical assurance the government of India place Cooch Behar in the list of states in the original constitution of India which was duly signed by the Hon'ble members of the constituent assembly of India on 26th November 1949 and accepted by the government of India on the same day. The Maharaja and people of Cooch Behar became really happy to know the news that Cooch Behar was included as a state in the original and final constitution of India for all round development of the people of Cooch Behar.

In this proper way the government of India wanted to stop the merger issue of Cooch Behar with west Bengal in constitutional way to save the ethnic people of Cooch Behar from the aggression of the government of west Bengal and where by to save the historical glory, economical, political and cultural standard of the people of Cooch Behar.

Sir,I earnestly pray to you to cancel this malafide merger of Cooch Behar with West Bengal. And it is also fact that by this merger, the government of west Bengal has been doing many harm to the ethnic people of Cooch Behar since the date of the malafide merger.

On this basis of above facts I on behalf of the people of Cooch Behar pray to you to kindly issue a mandatory order to the government of West Bengal to stop the administration of West Bengal over Cooch Behar and it's people and to take necessary action to recognize the status which the then government of india recorded Cooch Behar as a state with Union of India in the final and original constitution of India adopted by the government of India on 26th November, 1949 and this constitution came in force on 26th January, 1950 and declare Cooch Behar as a state with union of India before the coming loksabha Nirbachan with a view to give due respect to the constitution of India and the people of Cooch Behar. The area of this Cooch Behar state should be included the areas which the East India Company took from Maharaja of Cooch Behar.And by agreement which Maharaja of Cooch Behar got back when India became independent.

…nanking you

Yours faithfully,

President
Executive Committee
Greater Cooch Behar Democratic Party

SEPERATE STATE DEMAND COMMITTEE

পৃথক রাজ্য দাবী কমিটি

An Organization formed by –

The Greater Cooch Behar Peoples' Association , Greater Cooch Behar Democratic Party , All Koch Rajbongshi Students' Union , Kamtapur Peoples' Party , All Kamtapur Students'"Union , All Koch Rajbongshi Sahitya Sabha , All Assam Koch Rajbongshi Sanmiloni , Chilarai Sena & All Koch Rajbongshi Mohila Samiti

H.O.: Cooch Behar * B.O. : Bongaigaon

Biswajit Ray — ***Chairman***

Babuya Barman — ***Gen. Secretary***

Ref. No.: S.S.D.C. / 01/09 **Date: 29th Oct 2009**

<u>MEMORENDUM</u>

To,

The Excellency President of India
Rashtrapati Bhawan
New Delhi

Through The District Magistrate,

<u>Sub : " To create separate state in the name of Greater Cooch Behar or Kamtapur state ."</u>

Her Excellency ,

Under the reasonable necessity and acute socio-Economical , cultural and political crises , we the organizations , the Greater Cooch Behar peoples' Association , Greater Cooch Behar Democratic party , Kamtapur Peoples party , All Koch Rajbongshi Students Union , All Kamtapur Students Organization , Koch Rajbongshi Sahitya Sabha , All Assam Koch Rajbongshi Sanmiloni , Chilarai Sena & All Koch Rajbongshi Mohila Samiti Unitedly bound to hire your kind and sincere attention to the following facts for creating a new separate state in the name of Greater Cooch Behar or Kamtapur State .

I. Before British Rule in India , Maharaja Nara Narayan of Cooch Behar conquered all the small states of North Eastern India in 16th century and defended the North Eastern Border of India from foreign aggression in dignified way and protect all the small states of North Eastern India under the territory of India . The state of Cooch Behar was known in 16th century as Kamtapur State .

It is pertinent to mention that proposed area of Greater Cooch Behar or Kamatapur State was not the part of West Bengal and Assam . After gaining the Independence Cooch Behar State merged with Indian Dominion on 12th Sept. 1949 on the basis of Merger Agreement on 28th Aug. 1949 and which is adopted on 26th Nov. 1949 as a " C " category State in the India constitution .

II. When the Cooch Behar came to India , people of not only erstwhile kingdom but Whole of the areas regardless of their caste and creed were jubilant as they saw a ray of hope in making their homeland into a full-fledged state of Indian Republic . Then Prime Minister Pandit Jaharlal Neheru and Home Minister Sardar Vallabh Bhai Patel assured the people of the state , that their political and socio-economical aspiration would be fulfilled after joining the India . But in the year 1950 Cooch Behar "C " category state declared as a

(2)

district within State of West Bengal by Dr. B.C.Roy , the then Chief Minister of West Bengal . He did for the fear that creation of separate Cooch Behar state would definitely take away other districts of its own areas , which would further dismiss the size of West Bengal or Assam without taking any mended of the people of this area in 1956 . This kind of degradation of sate is a breach of trust , anti commitment and anti treaties .

III. That , Excellency the language , literature , culture of the people of the area are different from the language , literature and culture of West Bengal and Assam . Presently the indigenous People of the area has lost their glory , prosperity and happiness' ; to the contrary they are facing stark tragedy of repression , oppression , boundless exploitation in every sphere of there life.

IV. That , Excellency the proposed area is predominantly rural with over 80% of the population residing in the rural areas . Paddy , wheat etc are the major food grain grown in this region . Tea , jute the important commercial crops of India are produced in this region . But in fact that in spit of the wealth and variety of its natural resources , like forest , river etc. This region has remained industrially and agriculturally backward .

V. It's strange to say that there is a truth which is policy makers and decision takers of our country do not want to know and refused to understand that is killing , suppression and oppression of the indigenous people of the area is being carried out in the name of democracy . Law and order situation of the area is continuously deteriorating day by day . The indigenous people of the area extremely suffering and crying for gating justice of legal and constitutional rights of our country .

VI. That, Excellency our statehood parallel movements is running in the area after the Independence . In this regard Indefinite Dharna of the Greater Cooch Behar Peoples' Associations at Rashtriya Dharna Sthal , at Jantar Mantar , New Delhi is continuous since 28th Aug. 2006 to impress upon to the Govt. of India . Our struggle will continue till Greater Cooch Behar State or Kamtapur State is created under the union of India

The long pending demand of Greater Cooch Behar or Kamtapur State is historically proper , geographically desirable , economically essential , constitutionally correct and legally justified . In conclusion it is to be indicated that to emancipate the people of this vast region which includs six districts of North Bengal and fifteenth districts of Assam , a new state to be created in the name of Greater Cooch Behar or Kamtapur immediately nor we shall have no alternative than to launch greater democratic movement for the end of justice and redress .

In anticipation of your favorable action –

We remain ,
Yours faithfully

29/10/09

(BABUYA BARMAN)
General Secretary
Separate State Demand Committee

Correspondence Address :-
V.P.O. – G. Atiabari , P.S.- Dinhata
Distt. – Cooch Behar , 736135
India
Mobile - 919609836895

Yatha Dharma Tatha Jay

THE GREATER COOCH BEHAR PEOPLES' ASSOCIATION

H.O. : Prantik Bazar, Cooch Behar

General Secratary
Bangshi Badan Barman
Vill. & P.O. - Jarabari
Dinhata, Cooch Behar
Mob.: 9800512280

Central Committee

President
Dhirendra Nath Roy
Vill. Konamali
P.O. Maranadir Kuthi
Cooch Behar
Mob.:7602869912

Ref. No. Date 12-12-2014

SUB: DHARNA / RALLY AT JANTAR MANTAR (11TH & 12TH DECEMBER, 2014) FOR GRANT OF UNION TERRITORY (UT) STATUS TO COOCH BEHAR.

Respected Sir,

We would like to draw your kind attention to our last representations submitted to His Excellency, President of India, Memo No. –GCPA/RP/07, Home Minister of India, Memo No. GCPA/HD/07 and Hon'ble Prime Minister of India, Memo No. GCPA/PM/07 dated 07/11/14, where in we had once again pleaded for declaring UNION TERRITORY for Greater Cooch Behar Areas.

2. **Historical Background in Brief** : It is worth mentioning that the erstwhile Cooch Behar, one of the most important princely states of British India, categorized as class 'C' State under an agreement signed by Mr. Vapal Pangunni Menon, then Adviser to the Govt of India, Ministry of Stated by Mr. , Vapal Pangunni Menon, then Adviser to the Govt of India, Ministry of States, New Delhi on behalf of Union Govt. and Lt. Col. His Highness Maharaja Jagaddipendra Narayan Bhup BAhadur, the last king of Cooch Behar State The erstwhile subjects of the State were happy to be part of our nation. On the historic occasion of handing over of power, Honorable Home Minister, Sardar Vallabhbhai Patel sent a message to Sri Nanjappa, Chief Commissioner of Cooch Behar on the eve of formal handling over function wishing bright political future of ethnic Cooch Behar people.

Govt of India was expressed in Mr. V.P. Menon, then advisor to the Central Govt. vide His Demi official letter No.-F-15(19) P/40 dated the 30th August 1949 addressed to the Maharaja of Cooch Behar which categorically mentioned about the future status of Cooch Behar State. "**...It is the intension of the Govt. of India to administer for the present the territories of the Cooch Behar**

Jatha Dharma Tatha Jay

THE GREATER COOCH BEHAR PEOPLES' ASSOCIATION

H.O. : Prantik Bazar, Cooch Behar

General Secratary
Bangshi Badan Barman
Vill. & P.O. - Jarabari
Dinhata, Cooch Behar
Mob.: 9800512280

Central Committee

President
Dhirendra Nath Roy
Vill. Konamali
P.O. Maranadir Kuthi
Cooch Behar
Mob.:7602869912

Ref No. Date 12-12-2014

as a centrally administrated area under a Chief Commissioner ..." (Neheru patels correspondence 1945-55, vol-7 by Durga Das)

Unfortunately, the State was further got merged with West Bengal on 1st Jan. 1950 by then Chief Minister Late Dr. Bidhan Chandra Roy. After that hasty, tactful and wrongful merger with West Bengal, the political leadership West Bengal dominated by mainstream imported leaders never allowed the ethnic people or the erstwhile subjects of the State to see the light of development. Despite assurances given by Pandit Jawahar Lal Neheru, then Prime Minister and Sardar Vallabhbhai Patel, then Home Minister, these unfortunate people remained neglected in all aspects of their socio-economic, cultural, linguistic and most importantly remained deprived of true democratic right. Whatever, development can be seen in Cooch Behar today, it's fruits are being enjoyed only by those people who are non-ethnic people and got settled in our areas. Our ethnic people who form majority in rural areas are suffering from acute poverty, unemployment and getting displaced from urban areas.

3. **Demand No.1:** It is pertinent to mention here that during the deliberations of the last two 'Tripartite Meetings' held under patronage of home Ministry of Central Govt. and Govt. of Assam with the various organizations of Assam 03.09.2013 and 07.11.2013 respectively, we tried to project the various problems to the participating dignitaries of both Central as well as Assam Governments. We are thankful to Home Ministry for patient hearing to our problems during the meetings. Keeping in view of the constraints for grant of UNION TERRITORY this moment and considering the genuineness of our problems, we request your Excellency to restore the earlier status of Category 'C' Statehood to Greater Cooch Behar or grant Union Territory status to Greater Cooch Behar as per the Merger Agreement with adequate political safeguards to ethnic people with immediate effect.

4. **Demand No.2**: Our mother tongue is Rajbanshi, which is an old language and is spoken over two crore people in Greater Cooch Behar area and neighboring countries such Bangladesh and Nepal. Trace of this language can be found in old scriptures and writings such as 'Charjyapad' which were written much before advent of other contemporary language in Eastern and North eastern India. This Language was the official language of Cooch Behar Empire. However, due to political division of the area and non-recognition by the State, Rajbanshi language has not developed and this language is dying. With a view to save this language from getting extinct, immediate steps should be taken by

Jatha Dharma Tatha Jay

THE GREATER COOCH BEHAR PEOPLES' ASSOCIATION

H.O. : Prantik Bazar, Cooch Behar

General Secratary
Bangshi Badan Barman
Vill. & P.O. - Jarabari
Dinhata, Cooch Behar
Mob.: 9800512280

Central Committee

President
Dhirendra Nath Roy
Vill. Konamali
P.O. Maranadir Kuthi
Cooch Behar
Mob.:7602869912

Ref No. Date 12-12-2014

Govt. The language should be given constitutional recognition and included in the eighth schedule of the Constitution of India. We want immediate tabling of a Bill for constitutional recognition of Rajbanshi language.

5. **Demand No.3** : Immediate reorganization of the COOCH BEHAR RAJBANSHI SCHOOL which is providing education through the Rajbanshi language that leaded and guided by the Hindi and English from the primary stage. Because Rajbanshi Language is the requirement of not only for the ethnic people of the Greater Cooch Behar but also a national requirement of learning in mother tongue so the schools opened in some rural areas of the Greater Cooch Behar should be grant by the Central Govt. and grant the financial assistance to these schools and teachers.

6. **Demand No.4** : Post-Independence days could not be termed as happier as ought to be people of Cooch Behar kingdom, mainly the Rajbanshi speaking erstwhile subjects. The ex-Maharaja Lt. Colonel Jagadipendra Narayan Bhup Bahadur had been bitterly involved with legal battles. The significance of the articles of the agreement for merger signed between the Governor General of India and His Highness the Maharaja Jagadipendra Narayan Bhup Bahadur on 28th August 1949 was given a simple go by. An assurance was given to ex-Maharaja by V.P. Menon on behalf of the Central Govt. vide ministry of State letter D.O. No. F.15(19)/49 dated the 30th August 1949(PARA. No.14) saying that "the Government will Endeavour to associate absorption in the Indian Army". Therefore, we demand for raising of 'Narayani / Rajbanshi Regiment' as an infantry regiment in the Indian Army.

7. **Demand No.5** : Immediately set the legal president, Amithabh Narayan, to the Debottor Trust Board of Cooch Behar, which is illegally used by D.M. of Cooch Behar and fill up the two other posts of the Debottor Trust Board by the Native members of Cooch Behar in which – 1. Ambika Charan Roy & 2. Trikulendra Narayan were posted.

8. Demand No.6 : Complete the details of Amount of the Cooch Behar Development Fund for the native people of Cooch Behar, donated by the Maharaja Jagadipendra Narayan Bhup Bahadur of then Cooch Behar State immediately.

Jatha Dharma Tatha Jay

THE GREATER COOCH BEHAR PEOPLES' ASSOCIATION

H.O. : Prantik Bazar, Cooch Behar

General Secretary
Bangshi Badan Barman
Vill. & P.O. - Jarabari
Dinhata, Cooch Behar
Mob.: 9800512280

President
Dhirendra Nath Roy
Vill. Konamali
P.O. Maranadir Kuthi
Cooch Behar
Mob.:7602869912

Central Committee

Ref No. Date 12-12-2014

9. **Demand No.7** : The proper use of the Cooch Behar Development Fund in all over the Greater Cooch Behar area.

Keeping in view of the delay in grant of statehood from the Govt. side urgency in the matter genius ness of our problems, we are consider it appropriate for now to grant at least UNION TRERRITORY status to Greater Cooch Behar with adequate political safe guard with immediate effect, so that further deterioration in Sicio-Economic, Linguistic and political conditions of the ethnic people of erstwhile Cooch Behar can be stopped & Development work for our people can be taken up without further loss of time.

Therefore, sir we requested your good self to take up the matter strongly with the highest level for grant of UNION TERRITORY status for Greater Cooch Behar Area with immediate effect.

Yours faithfully,

Bangshi Badan Barman 12/12/14

(Bangshi Badan Barman)

General Secretary

General Secretary
The Greater Cooch Behar
People's Association

GOVERNMENT OF WEST BENGAL BACKWARD CLASSES WELFARE DEPARTMENT ADMINISTRATIVE BUILDING, DJ-4, SECTOR-II, SALT LAKE, KOL – 700091 WEBSITE: www.anagrasarkalyan.gov.in

No. 1896-BCW/6S-13/2017 dated the 7th June, 2017

Resolution

Whereas it is considered expedient to establish a Development Board for the Rajbanshi community of West Bengal, the Governor is hereby pleased to establish a Board by the name 'The West Bengal Rajbanshi Development and Cultural Board' with its Head Office in Cooch Behar, District Cooch Behar, West Bengal, under the administrative control of the Backward Classes Welfare Department, Government of West Bengal. This 'The West Bengal Rajbanshi Development and Cultural Board' shall be registered under the West Bengal Societies Registration Act, 1961 (West Ben. Act XXVI of 1961).

1. The aims and objects of the Board shall be:

   (a) To preserve, promote and safeguard folk art, folk music, folk dance and folk culture of the Rajbanshi community;

   (b) To promote education among the Rajbanshi community;

   (c) To publish or cause to publish literature, papers, books, research works, magazines etc. relating to customery rights, rituals, and other related literatures of the Rajbanshi community;

   (d) To support the Community for showcasing their identity and Culture;

   (e) To facilitate construction of houses, library, and museum for the Rajbanshi community;

   (f) To protect the historical and cultural landmarks, objects, structures, festivals of the Rajbanshi community;

   (g) To take up social welfare activities catering to the requirements of the Rajbanshi community;

   (h) To preserve and promote traditional Rajbanshi practices;

   (i) To facilitate works for protection of heritages of the Rajbanshi Community;

   (j) To do all such acts, deeds, matters and things connected thereto and therewith as may be necessary or deemed to be necessary as well as incidental or conducive to the foregoing objects.

2. The following shall be the authorities of the Board, namely, —

   (a) General Body and (b) Executive Body.

3. General Body. —

   (a) The General Body shall initially consist of not more than thirty-one (31) members to be nominated in the following manner: —

      (i) Chairperson — (to be nominated by the State Government in the Backward Classes Welfare Department from among the Rajbanshi community to be decided on the basis of recommendation of the largest recognised society or organization of the Rajbanshi community of West Bengal);

      (ii) Vice-Chairperson — (to be nominated by the State Government in the Backward Classes Welfare Department from among the Rajbanshi community to be decided on the basis of recommen-dation of the largest recognised society or organization of the Rajbanshi of West Bengal);

      (iii) Member-Secretary — One officer appointed by the State Government on deputation;

      (iv) Ex-officio member — District Magistrate, Cooch Behar or his representative;

      (v) Ex-officio member — District Welfare Officer, Backward Classes Welfare Department, Cooch Behar;

      (vi) Ex-officio member — Director, Cultural Research institute or his representative;

      (vii) other members to be nominated by the State Government from among the Rajbanshi community to be decided on the basis of recommendation of the largest recognised society or organization of the Rajbanshi of West Bengal.

   (b) Meeting of the General Body. —

   The General Body shall ordinarily meet at least twice a year on date, time and place to be fixed by the Secretary in consultation with the Chairperson and shall:

      (i) Adopt the annual report of the preceding year;

      (ii) Pass the audited accounts and budget estimates and;

      (iii) Transact any business as will be placed in the agenda suggested by the executive body.

(c) Extra-ordinary meeting. —

An extra-ordinary meeting of the General Body may be called by the Secretary, in consultation with the Chairperson and at the advice of the Executive body when needed to transact any special business or at the requisition signed by at least ten (10) members of the Board. The Chairperson shall convene the requisitioned meeting within thirty (30) days from the date of the receipt of the requisition. If the requisitioned meeting fails to attain quorum, it will not be adjourned and will be treated as failed.

Notice of the place, date and hour of any meeting and of the business to be transacted shall be issued to the members of the board at least seven (7) days before the date so fixed for the meeting.

(d) The following procedures shall be applicable to all the meetings of the General Body. —

(i) One-fifth of the members shall constitute the quorum. If there be no quorum, the meeting shall stand postponed to a date to be fixed by the Chairperson. A fresh notice shall be issued and if there be no quorum again those presents shall be competent to transact business.

(ii) The Chairperson or in his absence the Vice-Chairperson shall take the Chair. If neither the Chairperson nor the Vice-Chairperson be present the members present shall nominate a President for the meeting from amongst them and transact the business.

(iii) The power and duties of the General Body shall be as follows. —

(i) To provide guidelines of the activities of the board in conformity with the objects defined;

(ii) to consider and adopt annual report of the board;

(iii) to consider and approve the audited accounts and the budget estimates;

(iv) to appoint auditor for auditing the annual accounts.

4. Executive Body:

(a) The Executive body consisting of not more than eleven (11) members shall be constituted as following by the Government from amongst the members of the general body, namely,—

(i) Chairperson — to be nominated by the State Government in the Backward Classes Welfare Department from among the Rajbanshi community to be decided on the basis of recommendation of the largest recognised society or organization of the Rajbanshi of West Bengal;

(ii) Vice-Chairperson — to be nominated by the State Government in the Backward Classes Welfare Department from among the Rajbanshi community to be decided on the basis of recommendation of the largest recognised society or organization of the Rajbanshis' of West Bengal;

(iii) Member Secretary — One officer appointed by the State Government on deputation;

(iv) Ex-officio Member — District Magistrate, Cooch Behar or his representative;

(v) remaining 7 (Seven) members to be nominated by the State Government from among the Rajbanshi community to be decided on the basis of recommendation of the largest recognised society or organization of the Rajbanshis' of West Bengal.

Provided that the State Government in the Backward Classes Welfare Department may nominate such other persons, as it may consider necessary for smooth and proper functioning of the Board as members of the Executive body, who will also be members of the General Board.

(b) Meeting of the Executive body:

(i) The executive body shall ordinarily meet four times in a year and the quorum of such meeting shall be six (6);

(ii) An extra-ordinary meeting of the executive body may be called at the requisition of at least six (6) members of the Executive body to transact any special business. The requisitioned meeting shall be convened within fifteen (15) days from the date of receipt of the requisition. If the requisitioned meeting fails to attain quorum, it will not be adjourned and will be treated as failed;

(iii) Notice of all meetings of the executive body shall be issued at least seven (7) days before the date fixed for such meeting.

(c) The power and duties of the Executive body shall be as follows.—

(i) To manage the affairs of the body and for this purpose to constitute committees and / or sub-committees consisting of the members of the body and to frame and adopt such regulations, bye-laws and pass such orders as may appear conducive to and necessary for the efficient administration of the board and the attainment of these objects provided that such regulations shall not be repugnant to these regulations and shall be reported to the general body, the executive body will constitute a committee or sub-committee to be headed by the chairperson or the vice-chairperson for overall development of the Rajbanshi community;

(ii) To prepare and place before the general body and annual report, the audited accounts and the budget estimates;

(iii) To manage all the movable and immovable properties belonging to the board;

(iv) To acquire and accept in the name of the board any property (movable and immovable), articles, donations and gifts;

(v) To keep accounts audited and the budget estimate prepared, to do all other acts and deeds as shall be necessary and relevant in furtherance to the objects of the board;

(vi) To pay out of funds belonging to the board or out of any particular part of such fund, the expenses incurred by the board from time to time including expenses for the formation of the board and management of administration of the foregoing objects, including all rent, rates and taxes, outgoing and salaries, allowances including fringe benefits of the employees. The fringe benefit of the employees will be fixed in consultation with the Government.

(d) The Executive body shall exercise the power as mentioned above subject to the directives as may be issued by the State Government in Backward Classes Welfare Department from time to time.

(e) All the properties belonging to the Board shall be deemed to be vested in the Executive body but should be referred to as the properties of the Board.

5. The State Government in the Backward Classes Welfare Department shall make provision of fund for providing financial assistance to the Board.

6. Term of Office. —

The non-Government members may be nominated for a period of five years and their term will automatically expire on completion of five years. However, there is no bar to re-nominate any or all members for a further term or more.

7. Any member who is not a member in the ex-officio capacity shall cease to be a member of the Board if he or she fails to attend three consecutive meetings of the General Board.

8. Dissolution of Board. —

   The Board may be dissolved in accordance with the provisions under section 24 and 27 of the West Bengal Societies Registration Act, 1961. In the event of dissolution after satisfaction of all liabilities, all the assets including movable and immovable properties whatsoever that remain, shall vest in State Government who shall decide the future usage of them.

9. The West Bengal Societies Registration Act, 1961 (West Ben. Act XXVI of 1961) shall apply to this Board.

10. All matters related to Governing, the Board will be governed and guided by terms and conditions as laid down in the "Articles and Memorandum of Association" of the Board.

Ordered that the Resolution be published in the "Kolkata Gazette" and be circulated to all concerned.

By order of the Governor,
Sd/- S. K. THADE
Pr. Secy. to the Government of West Bengal.

No. 1896-BCW dated 07.06.2017, Source
https://wbxpress.com/west-bengal-rajbanshi-development-cultural-board/

Index

M

N

Y

Z